Praise for *Bigger than Bernie*

"An indispensable guide to twenty-first-century socialism from the viewpoint of clear-eyed, sharp-witted, smart, funny authors who lay bare the past failures of angry, narrow sectarianism, and offer a bold, dynamic vision for using the Sanders moment to build a stronger left. These authors, like the magazine they write for, give me hope!"

Jane McAlevey, author of *A Collective Bargain*

"Part history lesson, part guidebook; this is a love letter to the everyday people and movements who transformed this country, and who continue to declare that our lives have meaning and our future is worth fighting for. *Bigger than Bernie* isn't just about the man who's spent the majority of his political career on the fringes. It's about fighters. It's about thinkers. It's about love. It's about us."

Phillip Agnew, cofounder of the Dream Defenders

"Hannah Arendt said we should 'think what we are doing.' And that is what Meagan Day and Micah Uetricht have done here. Their book not only examines all that democratic socialists have achieved in the past few years but also gives an exhilarating account of what we'll be doing in the coming years. Anyone who thinks, with dread or relief, that the work comes to an end after Election Day in 2020 will think again. I'm going to keep coming back to them and their book in order to understand where and how it goes in the future."

Corey Robin, author of *The Enigma of Clarence Thomas*

"*Bigger than Bernie* is a comprehensive and necessary read for those longing for a more humane country, and as someone who has been up-close in many of our current fights for justice, I can attest to the power of its analysis. The authors champion non-reformist reforms that arise from and propel social movements, and provide an essential roadmap for achieving permanent change. An energizing and instructive account that brings socialism into the present tense."

RoseAnn DeMoro, former executive director of National Nurses United

"An urgent and essential text that forces us to think bigger than any one specific candidate about how to create a real and lasting politics of the multiracial working class. As chroniclers of both the Sanders campaign and the long history of class struggle, no one could better capture the promise and perils of this once-in-a-generation moment. I try never to miss a word that they write and you shouldn't either."

Krystal Ball, cohost of *Rising* on HillTV

"Day and Uetricht are two of the most brilliant and courageous intellectuals organically grounded in the marvelous militancy of the Sanders Movement. This indispensable book is a powerful, pioneering analysis of these new radical times, and a compelling vision of where it all might be going."

Cornel West, author of *Race Matters*

BIGGER THAN BERNIE

How We Go from the Sanders Campaign to Democratic Socialism

Meagan Day and Micah Uetricht

VERSO

London • New York

First published by Verso 2020
© Meagan Day, Micah Uetricht 2020

1 3 5 7 9 10 8 6 4 2

Verso
UK: 6 Meard Street, London W1F 0EG
US: 20 Jay Street, Suite 1010, Brooklyn, NY 11201
versobooks.com

Verso is the imprint of New Left Books

ISBN-13: 978-1-78873-838-5
ISBN-13: 978-1-78873-840-8 (UK EBK)
ISBN-13: 978-1-78873-841-5 (US EBK)

British Library Cataloguing in Publication Data
A catalogue record for this book is available from the British Library

Library of Congress Cataloging-in-Publication Data
A catalog record for this book is available from the Library of Congress

Typeset in Garamond by Biblichor Ltd, Edinburgh
Printed and bound by CPI Group (UK) Ltd, Croydon CR0 4YY

Contents

Introduction: Socialism in Our Time

Bernie Sanders has redefined what's possible in American politics.

The United States has long been thought to be a fundamentally conservative country, one where large numbers of people would never go for that scary, supposedly foreign "socialism." Pundits and historians have proposed many reasons why. Americans have had it too good, bought off by the overflowing abundance of this country. Socialist utopias have run aground "on the shoals of roast beef and apple pie," as Werner Sombart famously wrote in 1906. Or, when the point is raised that many Americans have always been poor and overworked and exploited and oppressed, observers have speculated that there's just something unique and undefinable about the American soul that makes us allergic to socialism. We're too competitive, too individualistic; cooperation just isn't in our nature. Not content with these explanations, leftists often focus on the singularly ferocious repression of labor and leftist organizing throughout US history and the successful division of the American working class through racism, sexism, xenophobia, and other forms of bigotry and oppression.

Whatever the reason, it's true that no socialist party has played a notable role in US politics for the better part of a century. Even after the 2008 financial crash, so clearly the result of a financialized capitalist system that drove the entire economy into the ground in reckless pursuit of profit, it was not the Left but the Right, in the form of the anti-taxation Tea Party, that saw an immediate resurgence. Eventually there was Occupy Wall Street, yet even at those left-wing protests, the concept of socialism remained on the margins. In the dominant culture, the principal use of the word "socialist" was as an absurd but powerful epithet thrown at decidedly non-socialist liberals like President Barack Obama. A mass socialist movement remained out of reach.

Bernie Sanders helped change that. He showed that there was actually a hunger in American life for a critique of capitalism when it was attached to a bold and credible policy agenda for wealth redistribution and working-class empower-ment. He called his politics "democratic socialism." Americans were supposed to be repelled by politicians like him who railed against millionaires and billionaires, and immune to exhortations to unite and fight along class lines. Yet here was a presidential candidate vying for the nomination of a major US political party, giving the party elite a run for their money, and putting class politics back on the map in the United States.

We owe Sanders a great deal for insisting and then prov-ing that a different kind of politics in the United States was possible. That contribution alone will likely reshape the US political landscape for decades to come, putting long-dor-mant left-wing ideas back into play. But as important as Bernie's politics and policy proposals are, they won't change the country and the world on their own. And they may not even be the most significant part of his legacy as a political figure.

What matters even more than Sanders's vision of socialism is the movement Sanders has helped set in motion. Sanders doesn't only argue for free public health care and college or a Green New Deal. He says we need a political revolution in this country to achieve those policies. The Sanders presidential campaigns have never been just about getting one man elected to the White House. They're about building a movement of millions that can long outlive and outperform any single electoral campaign.

So those of us who support Sanders and are inspired by his call for political revolution—and by the rise of other democratic socialist politicians like Representative Alexandria Ocasio-Cortez, the recent teachers' strike wave, the surge in the organized socialist movement, and everything else that has taken us all by surprise over the last few years—have to ask: What lessons should we draw from the Bernie Sanders moment? And how can we take all the energy that his candidacies have generated to build a movement that is bigger than a presidential candidate, bigger than a few dozen newly elected socialist representatives, and bigger than anything the US Left has seen in decades?

Not Me, Us

During one Democratic Party primary debate in June 2019, Bernie Sanders acknowledged that his opponents had some good ideas. Yet despite a preponderance of well-meaning plans, he asked, "How come nothing really changes? How come for the last 45 years wages have been stagnant for the middle class? How come we have the highest rate of childhood poverty? How come 45 million people still have student debt? How come three people own more wealth than the bottom half of America?"

He answered his own question. "Nothing will change unless we have the guts to take on Wall Street, the insurance industry, the pharmaceutical industry, the military-industrial complex, and the fossil fuel industry. If we don't have the guts to take them on, we'll continue to have plans, we'll continue to have talk, and the rich will get richer, and everybody else will be struggling."

Sanders was arguing that the missing ingredient is class struggle. It's the only way to actually realize plans that improve life for the majority of people at the expense of the tiny minority who currently run the show.

Sanders doesn't talk explicitly about what socialism means all that much. But it's clear from his advocacy of class struggle that he shares the broad outlines of a socialist analysis of what's wrong with capitalism. Capitalism is an economic system in which a small group of people own things like factories, companies, and money itself, and everyone else has to sell their labor to them in exchange for a wage, which they use to buy what they need to survive. Through their labor, workers create a surplus that is funneled into the bosses' pockets as profits rather than being used for the good of everyone.

The problem is that all of the capitalists' decisions are driven by profit. If they don't make enough of it, their enterprises collapse. And the easiest ways to maximize profit are to pay workers less, make them work harder, avoid regulations, skimp on taxes, and expand into new markets by doing things like privatizing public goods, all of which are bad for the working class. So these two classes are locked in struggle—and since the capitalist class is more powerful, the working class always gets the short end of the stick.

Under capitalism, the nation's (and the world's) tiny minority of economic elites has grown unfathomably rich by soaking up the wealth generated by working people while those working people's wages have remained stagnant and their lives have worsened. Those economic elites will not give up their power without a fight. The fight must be waged by millions of ordinary people, taking action at their jobs and at the ballot box, in the chambers and in the streets. Sanders's 2020 campaign slogan, "Not Me, Us," signals his intention to use his campaign to incorporate people into that fight, rather than merely convince them to vote for him on the basis that he's competent and morally upstanding.

At that same June primary debate, candidates were asked which single policy they would make a legislative priority if elected president. At that point Sanders already had a number of detailed flagship proposals, but he nonetheless rejected the premise of the question, saying, "We need a political revolution."

A political revolution is a tall order. But it's one we have some ideas about—ideas that have come from watching the massive groundswell of support for policies like Medicare for All and a Green New Deal; interviewing organizers and newly elected officials who aren't afraid to embrace those policies and use electoral campaigns to build the kind of bottom-up movements that Sanders has called for; seeing the surge in strikes and other kinds of militant labor organizing by workers across the country; witnessing the emergence of robust movements against the racism, sexism, and xenophobia that have been stoked by Trump but existed long before him; and participating ourselves in the new American socialist movement as members of the Democratic

Socialists of America and staffers for the socialist magazine *Jacobin*.

Nobody saw it coming, but the Sanders campaign has given us all a once-in-a-lifetime opportunity to transform our grotesquely unequal and unfair society, which is teetering on the brink of irreversible climate catastrophe. If we're going to seize that opening we'll need to build a mass, multiracial, working-class movement—one that's bigger, and more radical, than Bernie.

When we say that nobody anticipated the political transformations of the last few years in the United States, we include ourselves in the ranks of those taken by surprise. We've both had our ideas about what's politically possible in America radically transformed by the Sanders campaign—Meagan by becoming a socialist in the first place, Micah by realizing that socialism can actually become popular in America, the stuff of mass politics.

Sanders has showed us that socialist ideas don't have to remain fringe. If we talk about them the right way, millions of people will support them. In fact, given how miserable the status quo has become for so many, and given how dissatisfied so many people are with tepid, center-left solutions to our collective problems, huge numbers of people could be interested in socialism *precisely because* it is such a bold ideology. Maybe, we're at a moment when people are actually *hungry* for bold, uncompromising ideas from the Left—not terrified of them.

And not only have we learned that there is an appetite for Sanders's robust political program and an openness to his "democratic socialist" label, we've also learned that the alternative—advancing a feeble, centrist political program against a vigorous hard-right populism—doesn't work.

The entire argument made by liberals and some progressives in favor of running Hillary Clinton for president against Donald Trump in 2016 was that, while she was perhaps a less than ideal candidate given her long history of equivocation and occasionally outright reactionary politics, she would at least be the safe bet to defeat Trump, who represented a uniquely barbaric threat to the United States and the world. As everyone now knows, this "electability" argument turned out not to be true—the electable candidate was not elected. The Democrats' preference for this "safe" strategy over the years not only culminated in Trump's victory but has resulted in devastation up and down the ballot, from the halls of Congress to state houses and governorships throughout the country.

This failure on the part of the Democratic Party should shape how we approach electoral politics going forward. Americans are not excited by, and thus are not driven to vote for, candidates who defend the status quo. If Americans are going to reject the rabidly racist and xenophobic politics put forward by pro-corporate Republicans, they can't just be offered a slightly nicer, more diverse, less reactionary version by pro-corporate Democrats. They need a bold alternative political vision informed by clear moral principles that stands in stark contrast to what's on offer from Trump and the Right.

Sanders offered that in 2016, and the next generation of left-wing politicians and electoral organizers can offer it going forward, confident that running on a robust and uncompromising left-wing vision is not only morally correct, but strategically shrewd. The rise to prominence of first-term Congress members Alexandria Ocasio-Cortez, Ilhan Omar, and Rashida Tlaib is a promising sign that this message is getting through. Not only have they already shown a willingness to use their offices to advocate for the working class, but they have also so far resisted immense pressure to fall in line with the Democratic Party establishment. All three endorsed Sanders for president at the low point of his presidential campaign, when Sanders had suffered a heart attack and pundits rushed to declare that he was finished. If they remain steadfast, they will be anchors in the electoral wing of the movement Sanders started for decades to come. But just as we can't rely on Sanders alone, we can't rely solely on them either. We must take the reins ourselves.

We are convinced of the need for a political revolution in this country, and we think that revolution needs to be a democratic socialist one. By posing and answering key questions, this book will identify what that political revolution can look like and how we can continue to build it.

The first question we pose is: What exactly is so important about Bernie Sanders? We answer this by briefly tracing the history of socialism and class struggle in the United States, through periods of militancy and retreat, and showing how Sanders's own political trajectory was shaped by—but also stood outside of—that history. Somehow, through a wild amalgamation of left-wing politicization, a shrewd vision for how to operate independently from and outside the main currents of American politics, a uniquely stubborn personality, and perhaps a sprinkling of dumb luck, Sanders cut a distinct path through the decades, going from student socialist and civil rights activist to longshot third-party candidate to mayor of Burlington to member of Congress to serious presidential contender. His truly singular political perspective and personal attributes made him the perfect—and the only—candidate with the credibility and experience to provide political leadership for a new era of popular awakening and a rebirth of class politics.

Second, the question of how should we approach electoral politics is key. Elections are a major factor behind the current left resurgence, after all. There's a lot to learn from Bernie's presidential campaigns; the campaigns and in-office actions of public officials that have come in his wake, from Ocasio-Cortez in the House of Representatives to local elections like the six Chicago socialists who won election to city council; and even unsuccessful electoral campaigns that you may have never heard of, like the Jovanka Beckles campaign for California State Assembly. These kinds of electoral campaigns are essential to continue building the political revolution.

They are all examples of what we call "class-struggle campaigns," in which candidates openly identify as socialists, aren't afraid to name the enemy, and work to build working-class movements beyond their election—and beyond electoral politics altogether. Candidates who wage successful class-struggle campaigns will probably be in the political minority for the immediate future, but they can wield outsize influence by aggressively using their bully pulpit to promote socialist ideas. This book lays out some socialist strategies for punching above our weight.

We also talk about the Democratic Party, which has a monopoly on all electoral politics to the left of the Republicans, despite being an essentially centrist or occasionally center-left party. That monopoly distinguishes the American situation from that of almost every other country on earth—a major boon for the 1 percent and a disaster for the planet and the working class, both at home (under vicious attack by corporate power) and abroad (bearing the brunt of US imperialism).

The Democratic Party is a fundamentally pro-capitalist institution, and that is unlikely to ever change. But in the short and medium term, there are serious barriers to our scrapping the Democrats and creating a new mass party that can actually fight for the vast majority of society. That's why we argue for an approach to the Democrats that is willing to use the party's ballot line, preventing us from being doomed to complete political irrelevance, while laying the foundations for an eventual break with the party to create a future workers' party—what has been called a "dirty break" (as opposed to a "clean break") strategy.

We think that socialist organizations have a special role to play in building an independent working-class movement and eventually a party. They offer invaluable education, a coherent direction and common analysis for organizing around the most pressing issues of the day, a strategic orientation toward the working class, and a deep sense of comradeship and purpose. Right now, there's no better political home for those who want to join the fight than the Democratic Socialists of America, the country's largest socialist organization.

Socialists must have an inspiring long-term view of a revolutionized society, but also an actionable short-term agenda. We argue that there is great value in the struggle for reforms, if those reforms can advance socialist values and erode capitalists' power. Otherwise they're just tinkering around the edges and won't help build a bigger movement that can wage and win more ambitious fights down the line.

Finally, we argue that the labor movement is particularly important given the centrality of the working class in making the world function under capitalism, and the power workers can wield when they join together to fight the boss. A strong labor movement is one that is democratic and fights for the common good of all working-class people. The best way to build such a labor movement, as well as close the gap that currently exists between the socialist movement and the working class, is through what's called the "rank-and-file strategy," which places an emphasis on building power at the shop-floor level alongside other workers. In recent decades, some of the most dynamic and transformative fights in the labor movement have emerged because of this type of bottom-up, rank-and-file organization.

At the time of this writing, the fate of Sanders's bid for the presidency is uncertain. If he loses, the old problems remain, and the fight continues. If he wins, the fight is far from over: in fact it dramatically escalates, as the capitalist class will immediately seek to undermine our attempts to remake society. In both scenarios, the ability of the movement that has cohered around Sanders to stand on its own two feet and strategically exercise its power is the ultimate decisive factor. We conceive of this book as a guide for that movement as it strides into the future.

We have a once-in-a-lifetime opening to reshape the world for the many, not the few. In particular, given the impending reality of catastrophic climate change, we have no choice but to take advantage of this opening if don't want to live out our days in a dystopian nightmare. Capitalists are not only exploiting the vast majority of people and maintaining an order based on privatization and austerity that engenders needless suffering—they are also driving the planet to the brink of disaster. To pull it back from the precipice, we have to go toe-to-toe with the industries that are destroying the earth, which means our climate politics require a strong dose of class antagonism. If we want a habitable planet and a future for humanity, nothing less than democratic socialism will do.

Liberals are not taking the threats we face seriously enough. They've gotten caught up in sideshow spectacles rather than working to put forward an alternative to the grinding misery of life in America under capitalism. Sanders, meanwhile, showed that we aren't doomed to live in a world of inequality, oppression, and misery—that millions of people really are ready for a critique of the political and economic system we live under, and eager to create a society that's just, sustainable, and gives everyone a chance to flourish as human beings. The movement that his interventions have sparked, which is just beginning to find its footing, is our best hope for winning that society.

People often quote Werner Sombart's remark about the preponderance of "roast beef and apple pie," the incredible abundance that the US working class supposedly has access to, as a way to explain why socialism has not taken root here the way that it has elsewhere. Less quoted, however, is the ending of the 1906 book from which that line comes. Sombart, having given his full explanation for socialism's absence in the US, has this to say:

These are roughly the reasons why there is no Socialism in the United States. However, my present opinion is as follows: all the factors that till now have prevented the development of Socialism in the United States are about to disappear or to be converted into their opposite, with the result that in the next generation socialism in America will very probably experience the greatest possible expansion of its appeal.

Over a century later, these words ring true. We are in a rare, perhaps brief, window of political opportunity. Let's seize it to go beyond the Bernie Sanders campaign and win socialism in our time.

I

The Man and the Movement

Contrary to conventional wisdom about the viability of class politics in the beating heart of global capitalism, Bernie Sanders's rhetoric—calls for justice, equality, security, and shared prosperity in the form of free education, affordable housing, free high-quality health care, full employment, a secure retirement, and a clean environment for all—hasn't scared off masses of people. Instead, by polarizing politics along class lines, insisting that the reason many are denied these basic rights is that wealth and resources are captured by the top of society and kept there by design, Sanders has inspired the masses: 13.2 million voted for Sanders in the Democratic Party presidential primary in 2016, and his 2020 presidential campaign broke records for individual donations and volunteers.

Even his adversaries are often forced to respond to him— some, mostly Democrats, by half-heartedly adopting his popular demands in order to appeal to a constituency that is clearly moving left on key issues like Medicare for All; others, both Republicans *and* Democrats, by reviving the Cold War specter of authoritarian socialism to scare people into opposing an ambitious vision for social and economic change.

Socialism is now on the tip of the nation's tongue. In 2015, when Bernie first began running for president, it was the most-searched word on Merriam-Webster's online dictionary. Tens of thousands have joined the Democratic Socialists of America, and millions more talk about the merits of socialism over capitalism in conversations with their friends, families, and coworkers. Democratic socialist politicians are running and winning at the local, state, and national level. The sun is rising again on the idea that capitalism cannot provide the freedom and prosperity that it promises, and that the wealth created by all belongs to all.

What's most important about Sanders, however, isn't the policy ideas he's popularizing, or even his role in detoxifying the word "socialism." Yes, Medicare for All and tuition-free college as well as full medical and student debt cancellation would transform millions of lives. Likewise, the fact that socialism is no longer anathema has opened up new possibilities in politics (and has significantly increased socialist magazine subscriptions and socialist magazine employment, for which we are both grateful). But what matters most is how Bernie has promoted the idea that nothing he or any other candidate can do in office will win the kind of change we need without a political revolution of millions of people, a mass working-class movement taking to the streets and workplaces and fighting on its own behalf.

Sanders has played an important role in sparking that movement, and demonstrated that electoral politics shouldn't be seen as something contrary to or apart from its development. "He has absolutely infuriated the liberal establishment by committing a major crime," said Noam Chomsky in an interview with the *Intercept*. "It's not his policies. His crime was to organize an ongoing political movement that doesn't just show up at the polls every four years and push a button, but keeps working. That's no good. The rabble is supposed to stay home. Their job is to watch not to participate." Sanders's greatest contribution to American politics is that he continues to convince people that their own participation is necessary to win a better society.

If socialists had the opportunity to design the ideal scenario leading up to a viable democratic socialist presidential campaign, we would have scripted something very different. Ideally, a campaign like Sanders's would have been the culmination of a long path paved with many smaller victories. Socialism would already be a powerful movement in electoral politics, the workplace, and civil society, and the candidate would rise organically through the ranks of this dynamic, popular, and organized movement.

Unfortunately, both socialism and working-class movements were nowhere near ascendant when Sanders first ran for president. Instead, in a strange feat of reverse-engineering that few socialists saw coming, his campaign helped revive those movements.

After decades of marginalization and defeat, US socialist politics are entering a new era. When future histories of the American socialist movement are written, Sanders will play a prominent role. How does his life fit into the broader trajectory of the American Left?

On the one hand, Bernie's formative years aren't that different from many people his age on the Left. Born to a Jewish immigrant family (a demographic that has played key roles in the history of the American Left), he dove headlong into the political upheavals of the 1960s, joining the civil rights and socialist movements. As those upheavals subsided, he, too, retreated momentarily—to the idyll of rural Vermont. That story tracks closely to what we hear from many fellow travelers who were young and active during the last period of American social unrest and mass agitation.

On the other hand, especially after the 1970s, Sanders has managed throughout his career to stand both outside the main currents of the socialist movement and outside the American political mainstream. He has largely walked alone, remaining politically independent of the Democratic Party and avoiding its open embrace of neoliberal policies and abandonment of the labor movement, while also carving a successful path as an elected official. We should be grateful he did; otherwise, Sanders wouldn't have been able to hold the unique position he has held over the last four decades, culminating in his presidential runs and his contribution to the revival of socialist and working-class movements. Sanders's unique political biography has a lot to teach us about how to weather periods of left marginalization and defeat by remaining true to leftist principles—and how to strike again when the iron's hot.

Socialism and Sanders

Socialism has a long and storied history in the United States—never dominant, but at times popular and powerful.

Thomas Paine, one of the country's founding fathers (and its most radical), was an ardent critic of economic inequality and rule over the many by the few. Socialism didn't exist as an ideology in the late eighteenth century, but Paine believed in a society shaped by the ideals of democracy and equality, and even proposed the creation of proto—welfare state programs and taxing the rich. In the early nineteenth century, American utopian socialists inspired by thinkers like Robert Owen and Charles Fourier worked to create enclaves apart from society where labor was undertaken for the common good and not for profit, and where each community member had a say in the decisions that affected their lives. Those experiments didn't have much staying power, but they were important early efforts to realize the values of socialism in the United States.

As the Industrial Revolution progressed and the world saw the rise of an industrial working class toiling in factories and mills, especially throughout Europe and the United States, Karl Marx and Friedrich Engels began writing, arguing that those workers had both the strategic power in society as well as the material self-interest to fight for and win socialism. In the second half of the nineteenth century, workers throughout the United States, many of them influenced by Marx and Engels's theories but most simply interested in winning better lives for themselves and their families, began organizing unions to fight for dignified working conditions and fair pay—and waging some of the bloodiest battles in all of world history against bosses, police, and even soldiers.

Those battles ebbed and flowed past the turn of the twentieth century, with major strikes and union organizing kicking off in railroads, steel factories, and other industries, and even citywide general strikes like the one in Seattle in 1919. The Socialist and Communist parties also grew during this time, with the socialists electing over a thousand officials all over the country—from the "sewer socialists" who led Milwaukee, Wisconsin, for decades to two members of the US Congress.

The most prominent socialist political leader during the first decades of the twentieth century was Eugene V. Debs, whom Bernie Sanders cites as a personal hero. (Sanders made a documentary about Debs in the 1970s, and reportedly has a framed portrait of Debs in his office in Washington, DC.) Debs led militant strikes as an officer with the Brotherhood of Locomotive Firemen and Enginemen, prompting the *New York Times* to denounce him as "a lawbreaker at large, an enemy of the human race" in 1894. He first read the works of German socialists like Marx, Engels, and Karl Kautsky when he was imprisoned for his role in organizing a strike. Thereafter, he devoted himself to the cause not just of unionism, but of socialism.

Debs ran for president on the Socialist Party ticket five times—at his most successful in 1912, he won 6 percent of the popular vote. But Debs was steadfast in his belief that the task of the Socialist Party was not merely to win votes. It was to awaken the American working class and create an independent electoral expression of class struggle happening on the ground. "I would not lead you into the promised land if I could, because if I led you in, someone else would lead you out," Debs said—a sentiment echoed in Sanders's campaign slogan "Not Me, Us" over a century later. Victory for workers would remain elusive unless workers organized themselves.

In 1918, Debs was arrested for speaking out against World War I. The country had been whipped into a pro-war hysteria, and federal authorities charged him with intending to "cause and incite insubordination, disloyalty, mutiny and refusal of duty in the military," and for trying "to obstruct the recruiting and enlistment service of the United States." He knew that his antiwar agitation would likely result in his imprisonment, but he did it anyway, telling a crowd gathered in Canton, Ohio, "The master class has always declared the wars; the subject class has always fought the battles."

Debs ran for president for a final time from behind bars in 1920, receiving, incredibly, over nine hundred thousand votes. But his incarceration delivered a blow to his health from which he never recovered. He died a few years later, in 1926.

For nearly a century, no American socialist has proven as popular a leader as Debs—not until Sanders began his first campaign for president in 2015. Debs was an important inspiration for Sanders, not just because of Debs's socialist politics, but because of the way he communicated them. Debs's biographer Nick Salvatore writes that he "remains the classic example of an indigenous American radical. He was not born a Socialist, and he did not reject American values when he became one." Sanders, too, would speak about socialism in distinctly American tones, combatting the widespread notion that socialism is an exclusively foreign concept that could never take root in American soil—while also remaining critical of the role of the United States in perpetuating war and inequality around the world.

Shortly before Sanders was born, another burst of labor militancy kicked off. During the Great Depression, workers struck in enormous numbers. In 1934, San Francisco, Minneapolis, and Toledo, Ohio, all saw massive general strikes, while autoworkers in Flint, Michigan, famously sat down on the job and occupied their factories a few years later. This period led to the explosive growth of the labor movement. Communists, socialists, and other leftists played key roles in these fights. And elected socialists were still around too—including one, Vito Marcantonio, who was representing East Harlem in Congress at the very moment Bernie Sanders was born a few miles away in Brooklyn.

That explosion of working-class organizing was the impetus behind President Franklin Delano Roosevelt's New Deal, the massive (and at times contradictory) project that remade American life in the 1930s and vastly improved the material well-being of millions of people throughout the country. Socialists and Communists would play key roles in every aspect of the New Deal, from organizing the working-class upheavals that spurred Roosevelt to pass pro-worker legislation to even working in some of the newly created New Deal agencies under Roosevelt. While Jim Crow white supremacy, sexism, and other oppressions weren't ended by the New Deal, and some of the new labor reforms actually helped tame expressions of working-class militancy, the New Deal would become an important reference point for Sanders's own politics over half a century later—showing, at the very least, that it was possible to undertake a massive mobilization to extend social rights at the federal level.

Sanders was born while Roosevelt was still president, on September 8, 1941, in Brooklyn, New York, to Jewish parents. His father had immigrated from Poland, and his mother's parents were from Poland and Russia. The family was not impoverished, but money was a constant struggle for his paint salesman father and the entire Sanders household. "It wasn't a question of putting food on the table. It was a question of arguing about whether you buy this or whether you buy that," Sanders recollects. "I remember a great argument about drapes—whether we could afford them."

Sanders has contrasted his upbringing in a rent-controlled apartment to that of Donald Trump, who is roughly his same age and also grew up in New York City. "I did not have a mom and dad who gave me millions of dollars to build luxury skyscrapers and casinos and country clubs," he has said. "But I had something more valuable: I had the role model of a father who had unbelievable courage in journeying across an ocean, with no money in his pocket and not knowing a word of English."

Sanders's father had left Poland in 1921. "He came to escape the crushing poverty that existed in his community," Sanders explains, "and to escape widespread antisemitism. Needless to say I would not be with you today if he had not made that trip from Poland because virtually his entire family there was wiped out by the Nazis."

Bernie grew up in a milieu that was given to left-wing politics. His parents weren't radicals—more like New Deal Democrats, who according to Bernie's brother, Larry, "understood that the government could do good things." But many Jewish European immigrants *were* radicals, playing key roles in the labor movement and in the Communist and Socialist parties and other radical organizations in the first half of the twentieth century. Those immigrants' children and grandchildren often went on to play a sizable role in radical politics in the century's second half. When McCarthyism and the Red Scare kicked off not long after Sanders's birth, many reds who were expelled from the labor movement and blacklisted from the entertainment industry were descendants of Jewish immigrants.

Sanders's mother died when she was forty-six after a difficult bout of illness. This experience was Sanders's first brush with the intrusion of financial worry into people's most private, painful moments, leading eventually to his embrace of national health insurance. As a *New York Times* reporter writes, "As his mother's health declined and his family struggled to pay for medical treatment, he was spending more time attending to her than in classes at Brooklyn College, suffering through what his brother called 'a wrecked year' leading to her death." After that year, Sanders transferred from Brooklyn College to the University of Chicago. His father died almost immediately thereafter, in 1962.

Newly parentless, Sanders found his footing in Chicago just as the student and civil rights movements took center stage in the country's politics. Student activists like him were important drivers of the upsurges of the sixties, joining the civil rights movement's efforts to win voting rights and end Jim Crow, and fighting the Vietnam War. Bernie was "radicalized by the grinding poverty he saw for the first time in places such as the city's South Side." He later described his time in Chicago as "the major period of intellectual ferment in my life."

Sanders joined the civil rights movement in Chicago. In 1962, as the president of his college's chapter of the Congress of Racial Equality (CORE), he led a sit-in at the University of Chicago. For thirteen days, student members of CORE occupied the university president's office to demand the school end its policy of housing segregation in the off-campus buildings it owned. The administration agreed to create a committee to look into the issue, but according to Sanders at the time, this was not sufficient to resolve "an intolerable situation when Negro and white students of the university cannot live together in university-owned apartments." CORE continued to pressure the university, picketing its buildings that refused to rent to African Americans.

In 1963, the University of Chicago finally gave in and ended its racist housing policy. But the struggles for racial justice in Chicago weren't over. Months later, Sanders joined a protest against racist education policies in Chicago. Starved of public investment, crowded black schools were being supplied with temporary trailers to use as classrooms. Sanders went to protest the installation of these trailers and was arrested on the spot, his legs chained to those of black protesters. He was taken to jail, and bailed out by the NAACP. His arrest was captured by a photographer for the *Chicago Sun-Times*, his face in a grimace as police drag him away from the protest.

Later that year, Sanders traveled to Washington, DC, to attend the March on Washington for Jobs and Freedom, where Dr. Martin Luther King Jr.—Bernie's other personal hero—gave his famous "I have a dream" speech. Many Americans remember the line from that speech about not judging people by the color of their skin but instead by the content of their character. Few remember that King praised the "marvelous new militancy which has engulfed the Negro community" and warned that "the whirlwinds of revolt will continue to shake the foundations of our nation until the bright days of justice emerge."

At the helm of key positions in the civil rights movement were socialists like A. Philip Randolph, who had cut his teeth in the Socialist Party and as the leader of the Brotherhood of Sleeping Car Porters, and Bayard Rustin, whose activist life included stints in the antiwar movement, Communist Party, and Socialist Party. Even King called himself a democratic socialist. He had been recruited to the Montgomery Bus Boycott campaign by a labor organizer, E. D. Nixon, who had honed his politics and skills in the Brotherhood of Sleeping Car Porters. King's final speech, the night before he was murdered, was delivered to Memphis sanitation workers who were on strike.

The socialist traditions of mass action and of struggle from below were also integral to the civil rights movement's strategy. That movement overturned the white-supremacist Jim Crow order not simply by electing politicians sympathetic to civil rights (though it did that, too), but also by marching, getting arrested in civil disobedience actions, launching boycotts, and going on strike. Sanders's participation in the most important American social movement of the twentieth century helped shape his views on the necessity of mass movements to win social change.

"My activities here in Chicago taught me a very important lesson that I have never forgotten," Sanders said at a 2019 rally in front of 10,000 people in the city. "Real change never takes place from the top on down. It always takes place from the bottom on up."

In Chicago, Sanders's activities were not restricted to the civil rights movement. He also joined the Young People's Socialist League (YPSL), the youth section of the Socialist Party. "It helped me put two and two together, in my mind," Sanders said later about his time in the YPSL. "We don't like poverty, we don't like racism, we don't like war, we don't like exploitation. What do they all have in common? . . . What does wealth and power mean? How does it influence politics?"

This early experience with the socialist movement clearly made a deep impression—so deep that Sanders persisted in calling himself a socialist for the rest of his life, through all the decades during which the term was toxic. That persistence in claiming the socialist label led many to write him off as an eccentric over the years, but by refusing to give it up, Sanders helped popularize socialism decades later. His political steadfastness and stubbornness paid off.

When Sanders left the University of Chicago, he never rejoined a socialist group (though he did occasionally give speeches, for example, at Democratic Socialists of America conventions). But you can see the perspective he gained from joining that group stamped on his entire subsequent political career.

One thing Sanders inherited from the socialist tradition is a fundamental belief that the rich are not your friends, that we need to combat the wealthy and powerful rather than cozy up to them to make social change happen. Because a small number of elites benefit from our political and economic system as it is, Sanders believes they will never voluntarily give it up. The way to advance the interests of the vast majority is *through* conflict, not around it.

His rhetoric identifies social problems, then names the small group of powerful people who are creating those social problems, and says we have go to battle against them. That rhetoric stands in stark contrast to the dominant approach of the Democratic Party, even of its "progressive" wing, which is reticent about that need to name and shame and fight and dispossess the great hoarders of wealth in our society. Consider the difference between Sanders and the progressive 2020 Democratic presidential candidate Elizabeth Warren. She said on the Democratic Party presidential debate stage in 2019, "I don't have a beef with billionaires," before suggesting they "pitch in." The Sanders campaign, by contrast, made bumper stickers emblazoned with the words "Billionaires should not exist." Warren's approach assumes that the ultra-rich can continue to exist without distorting our politics or immiserating wide swaths of the country. Sanders says the ultra-rich can't stay ultra-rich.

While Sanders clearly thinks he has an important and unique role to play in the fight for a better world as a high-profile politician, he also constantly emphasizes that the election of one person, even one who has solid political and moral commitments to fight for the many, not the few, isn't enough to change the world. To do that, we need a mass movement of working-class people. The power of the capitalist class is immense; to overcome it, we need to not just win elections but collectively assemble as millions of people marching in the street, engaging in strikes and boycotts, pressuring politicians, and pushing back against the inevitable retaliation for our victories. This is the socialist argument about how progressive change happens under capitalism: not through the independent actions of benevolent leaders, but by the working class coming together as a class and fighting for itself.

Could Sanders have developed this kind of analysis about the way change occurs under capitalism without joining a socialist organization and participating in a mass grassroots movement? It's possible, but highly unlikely. Both endeavors give their members and participants a political education about how the world works and a base of experience in making that social change happen that is not found elsewhere. These experiences shaped Sanders's conception of power in society and sharpened his clarity about which side he was on.

Against the Current

In 1968, the zenith of the decade's activism, Sanders moved to Vermont. The New Left felt like it was on the march forward; in hindsight, we know that it would soon go into decline. In some ways, Sanders was ahead of the curve. Before the rest of the movement petered out, he became "captivated by rural life" and headed northeast. Many would eventually follow suit, whether to other rural idylls, urban progressive enclaves, or just away from their previous lives as activists.

Bernie didn't hold a "real job" for years—a biographical detail that opponents try to wield as a cudgel, but which probably resonates with rather than repels downwardly mobile young people today. He made documentaries that he sold to schools and universities, and occasionally wrote for alternative newspapers. Sanders gives a rosy, even petty capitalist gloss to those years in later tellings of his life's story: in *Our Revolution*, he calls his radical filmmaking "a reasonably successful small business."

His friends tell a different story. He was evicted from one apartment, his electricity turned off at another. A friend of his at the time told a journalist in 2015 that Sanders worked a bit as a carpenter, but "he was a shitty carpenter." He was on unemployment benefits for a while, and was living "just one step above hand to mouth," another said. Hardly the typical life plan of an aspiring future president.

Sanders eschewed material possessions, a "real job," and a stable existence. This wasn't much different than many of his generation post–New Left. The upsurges of the student, civil rights, and antiwar movements began to wane in the 1970s, and some former activists sought personal and political fulfillment by heading "back to the land," trying to create new, egalitarian worlds by leaving mainstream society behind, sometimes on rural communes, in states like Vermont. Sanders was no hippie, but much as the 1960s movements shaped him into a socialist and activist, the disillusionment of the 1970s shaped him, briefly, as a kind of dropout.

But it is here that Sanders began swimming against the main currents of the Left at the time. At a time when many others in his demographic had begun swapping protest signs for fermentation cookbooks, Sanders's passion for politics found its first electoral expressions. Shortly after arriving in

Vermont, he decided to run for Senate and then governor on the ticket of a small, left-wing third party in Vermont, the Liberty Union Party, in 1972. He ran for Senate again on the Liberty Union ticket in 1974, and then for governor again in 1976.

This wasn't the path chosen by someone who valued winning political power above all else. He never cracked double digits in these elections. But even while reflecting on those campaigns years later, Sanders had no regrets. "The issues that I and other Liberty Union candidates raised during that campaign helped play an important part in the election results and eventually resulted in changes in public policy," he wrote in his first book, referring to issues, such as property tax reform and better provision of dental care for poor children, which were eventually taken up by the Democratic winner of the governor's race. "Despite our [winning] a paltry one percent [of the vote], the Liberty Union made an impact on major legislation."

This was a repeat of a scenario that had played out in high school, when Sanders ran for student body president and lost, only to watch the victor adopt his proposal for the school to raise funds for Korean War orphans. And it also foreshadowed what happened in 2016, when Sanders's first presidential campaign came up short but nonetheless caused a massive political sea change. Sanders has won plenty of campaigns— but crucially, the ones he's lost have also moved the needle.

His tenure with the Liberty Union Party gives us another glimpse at how deeply the demands and vision of socialism informed his politics. The Liberty Union Party called for mass decommodification and nationalization. "I favor the public ownership of utilities, banks and major industries," he said in one interview in 1973. On another occasion, Sanders wrote an open letter to one of his state's senators, published in a Vermont newspaper:

> I would also urge you to give serious thought about the eventual nationalization of these gigantic companies. It is extremely clear that these companies, owned by a handful of billionaires, have far too much power over the lives of Americans to be left in private hands. The oil industry, and the entire energy industry, should be owned by the public and used for the public good—not for additional profits for billionaires.

"We have got to begin to deal with the fact that corporations do not have the god-given right to disrupt the lives of their workers or the economic foundation of their towns simply because they wish to move elsewhere to earn a higher rate of profit," he said in a press release in 1976. In that press statement, he floated the idea of capital controls, where the state blocks the free movement of capital, prohibiting businesses from moving elsewhere and taking jobs and the economic life of a region with them. Capital controls, decommodification, nationalization—these are radical ideas, and they testify to Sanders's roots in the socialist movement.

Sanders left the Liberty Union Party in 1977, frustrated that it was too narrowly focused on elections. "The function of a radical political party is very simple," he said in his resignation letter. "It is to create a situation in which the ordinary working people take what rightfully belongs to them. Nobody can predict the future of the workers' movement in this country or the state of Vermont. It is my opinion, however, that if workers do not take power in a reasonably short time this country will not have a future."

Perhaps if Sanders had lived in a country with an electoral system that didn't maintain a two-party stranglehold, he would have found electoral success earlier. Jeremy Corbyn, the former British Labour Party leader to whom Sanders is often compared, holds similar politics to Sanders and has a similar history of involvement in important leftist movements throughout his life, from solidarity campaigns against apartheid in South Africa to opposing wars. He got involved in electoral politics just after Sanders, but Corbyn had a labor party to join; when Sanders was on the margins of Vermont politics with the Liberty Party, Corbyn won his first elections for Labour.

Radicals in the United States have long wrestled with the question of what to do about the Democrats, a party that has never come anywhere close to being a true workers' party, and has always made compromises with capitalists that prevent it from embracing a full-on fight for the working class (a question we will take up at length in Chapter 4). Neither of the two basic choices has been good: stifle your criticisms of the party and join them, viewing the Democrats as the only game in town and the only party through which you can get anything done; or stick to your principles and work through third parties that never win. The former has been a recipe for conservatizing progressives and socialists; the latter, a recipe for political marginalization and demoralization.

Sanders, however, managed to largely avoid the pitfalls of both and blaze his own independent political path.

Leaving the Liberty Union Party did not spell the end of Sanders's involvement in politics. He ran for mayor of Burlington as an independent in 1980 and won—the same year Ronald Reagan captured the presidency and the Right saw a national upsurge. Sanders's eight years as Burlington mayor are a fascinating study in local left governance. He won office by a mere ten votes, and immediately set to work using his position to improve living standards for average Burlingtonians.

His list of accomplishments as mayor is long. At a time when so much of the country was moving rightward, Burlington under Sanders's mayorship raised taxes on wealthy developers, expanded affordable housing (which included the establishment of a pioneering community land trust), fought for rent control, supported municipal workers' unions, expanded public funding for youth programming and the arts, fought utility companies, instituted feminist measures in local government, outlawed discrimination in housing, became one of the first cities to hold an official Gay Pride parade, and stopped a massive condominium development from taking away a large plot of public land on Lake Champlain.

But his tenure didn't just focus on local issues. Nationally, Sanders spoke out consistently against Reagan's savage budget cuts. He also used the small city's mayoral office to speak out against the president's blood-soaked interventions in Central American countries like Nicaragua and El Salvador. After the Sandinista revolution in Nicaragua overthrew the country's brutal Somoza dictatorship, the Reagan administration backed the Contras, a group of right-wing militants responsible for destroying the country's infrastructure, numerous rapes and sexual assaults against Sandinista supporters and other Nicaraguans, and mass bloodshed across Nicaragua.

In El Salvador, the United States sought to avoid a similar revolution by propping up a brutal, bloodthirsty right-wing dictatorship that could claim almost no backing from the Salvadoran people themselves. The result was some of the worst human rights atrocities ever committed in the Western

Hemisphere, including the assassination of Archbishop Óscar Romero while he gave mass in 1980; numerous massacres of innocent civilians in villages like El Mozote, where nearly a thousand were slaughtered, and the rape and murder of four American churchwomen, both in 1981; the massacre of six Jesuit priests along with a housekeeper and her daughter at the Central American University in 1989; and a constant stream of bullet-riddled, tortured bodies that piled up on streets throughout the country.

The Central America solidarity movement was nowhere near the size of the civil rights movement or the movement against the Vietnam War, but it was an important movement across the United States opposing Reagan's foreign policy. Typically, few mayors weigh in on foreign policy issues of any kind, but Sanders held numerous Central America solidarity teach-ins and rallies in Burlington. In 1982, he spoke at a rally of hundreds at City Hall against US intrusion in El Salvador, and pushed a ballot initiative against intervention in the country. He also established a sister city program with Puerto Cabezas, Nicaragua, and even went to Managua, Nicaragua, as mayor and attended a pro-Sandinista rally in 1985.

"I plead guilty to, throughout my adult life, doing everything that I can to prevent war and destruction," Sanders told the *New York Times* in 2019 after the paper attacked his mayoral record on Central America. "As a mayor, I did my best to stop American foreign policy, which for years was overthrowing governments in Latin America and installing puppet regimes. I did everything that I could as a mayor of a small city to stop the United States from getting involved in another war in Central America trying to overthrow a government."

All this history is worth revisiting not just for what it says about Sanders's approach to governance, but also for what it suggests about how newly elected left officials can approach their time in office. Regardless of whether an official is a small-town mayor, city council member, or a member of the House or Senate, it's possible to use their elected office to both pursue a robust, pro-working-class agenda for their immediate constituencies and speak out against the reactionary policies that benefit the wealthy few and hurt the many, as well as join movements against imperialist bloodshed around the world. Sanders managed to do all of the above as Burlington's mayor, at a time when the Right was in power across the country.

During this time and afterward, Sanders was not a member of any party, formally accountable to no one but himself—and still he managed to blaze a trail to political success that would eventually lead to two presidential campaigns. In the annals of astonishing and improbable American political success stories, Sanders's ranks high.

When Sanders first won Burlington's mayoral election, neoliberalism had taken hold of US politics. Neoliberalism is the economic philosophy, hatched in the mid-twentieth century—but finding expression beginning in the 1970s and increasing in the 1980s—that held that the majority's needs could best be served by allowing private capitalist markets to expand into every crevice of society. For neoliberals, state interventions in the affairs of business are only desirable insofar as they buttress this expansion, ensuring maximum profits for business owners. This is justified by the "trickle-down economics" theory advanced under Ronald Reagan's presidency, which posits that profits for the wealthy are naturally reinvested into society, creating

brighter opportunities for all further down the economic
ladder.

Neoliberalism imagines workers as entrepreneurs, selling
their labor as a commodity the way a business sells commodities, in an environment of supposedly free exchange, not
skewed by power imbalances or marred by exploitation. The
winners in this exchange are simply the most successful entrepreneurs. Neoliberalism thus promotes the idea of meritocracy:
the best players always win the game, and wealth and success
are proof of inherent talent and superiority. Collective bargaining rights, the welfare state, and redistribution of wealth
represent unfair compensation to the undeserving losers. If
you want a better life, work and innovate harder.

The rise of neoliberalism has been disastrous for workers
in the United States and helped defeat and dismantle the
movements that won so many gains in the New Deal era and
the 1960s. It broke the strength of American unions, as
employer attacks (combined with conservative strategies by
unions themselves) led to concessions like cutbacks in pay,
benefits, and working conditions, and eroded workers' faith
and investment in their own unions. Since the dawn of this
process in the 1970s, American workers' wages have remained
relatively flat, while productivity has soared—at six times the
rate of worker pay. Capitalists' profits, meanwhile, have likewise skyrocketed. Austerity has been the order of the day,
with tax giveaways for the wealthy, massive cuts to already
meager welfare benefits, privatization of public goods, and
erosion of workers' rights.

In the latter decades of the twentieth century, Democrats
became enamored of neoliberalism. If Sanders had chosen to
pursue a political career through the party, he might have
been forced to accommodate their worldview—especially

without a left-wing working-class movement at his back of the type that is beginning to reemerge today. Luckily for us all, he chose another path.

Outsider in the House

Bernie Sanders graduated from the mayorship to run for Vermont's sole House of Representatives seat, winning in 1990. The first words out of his mouth, just minutes after he discovered he was going to be a national politician, were:

> You all understand that it is not going to be Bernie Sanders or any other member of Congress that's going to bring about the change that we need. What we need in this country is a mass movement of tens of millions of people who are prepared to stand up and say we want national healthcare. We want the millionaires and the multinational corporations who have not been paying their fair share of taxes to start paying. We want money going into education and environmental protection. And no more Star Wars [Reagan's boondoggle missile defense program] or stealth bombers.

He became the only political independent in the House at that time, striking a deal with the Democratic leadership to remain outside the party but caucus with them and receive committee assignments according to his seniority as if he were a Democrat (though last in line in his class of representatives). That deal again reflected his special ability to thread the needle of maintaining political independence from both the Democrats and Republicans while avoiding political marginality.

Meanwhile, the Left as a whole was still lost in the wilderness. Neoliberalism was already on the ascent by the time the Berlin Wall fell in 1989 and the Soviet Union collapsed in 1991. Those events prompted wild celebrations of the free market and led to what Francis Fukuyama called "the end of history"—capitalism had won. Critiques of inequality were passé, greed was good, and there was no alternative. Attacks on the American working class intensified. Social welfare programs were being eviscerated nearly as zealously by Democrats like President Bill Clinton as by his Republican predecessors Reagan and George H.W. Bush. The labor movement was under assault, with unionization and strike rates dropping steadily. The progressive causes to which Sanders had dedicated his life were losing ground.

Still, he stayed busy in the House. Sanders opposed the first Gulf War. He fought the brutal "welfare reform" bill—led by the Republicans but supported by many Democrats, as he noted at the time. He spoke out against executives' bonuses at Lockheed Martin. He decried the racism, sexism, xenophobia, and homophobia of the rightward-moving Republican Party under Representative Newt Gingrich's leadership as Speaker of the House in the last half of the 1990s. He was one of the cofounders of the House Progressive Caucus in 1991. And as he would for the rest of his career, he fought for a single-payer health care system.

Sanders often brought righteous anger to the House floor. In a speech in 1992, he said:

> In case you don't know, and you haven't seen the latest polls, the American people hold the president of the United States in contempt, they hold this institution in contempt, they hold the Republican Party in contempt, they hold the

Democratic Party in contempt . . . We are spending $270 billion a year on the military, but we don't have a major enemy. I know it hurts your feelings. I know you're upset about it. I know you're hoping and praying that maybe we'll have another war. Maybe somebody will rise up. But it ain't happening. The Soviet Union doesn't exist! The Warsaw Pact is through! Who you worried about? Iraq? Panama? Who you worried about? I'll tell ya who I'm worried about. I'm worried about the fact that our workers are seeing a decline in their standard of living. They want to see our industry be rebuilt . . . The American people want to see our kids educated. They want a Head Start program. They want their kids to be able to go to college. They want to wipe out the fact that 5 million children in this country go to bed hungry. They want childcare for their kids. They want decent education. Let's have the guts to give some leadership to this country. The Cold War's over. Let's reinvest in America.

Sanders's tenure in the House spanned sixteen years. Those years were bleak ones for the Left, regardless of who held the presidency. The anti-corporate globalization movement started picking up steam in the mid-1990s under President Bill Clinton, and reached its zenith when it shut down the 1999 World Trade Organization meeting in Seattle through mass protest. The trade deals protesters were criticizing, which gutted democracy in the United States and around the world and hurt workers both at home and abroad, have long been the target of Sanders's criticism.

But the movement's momentum evaporated after the terrorist attacks of September 11, 2001. The Bush administration beat the drums of war, first mobilizing to invade

Afghanistan—which, in a lapse of judgment Sanders did support, along with every member of the House but one, California's Barbara Lee—then mobilizing in 2002 to invade Iraq. Millions around the country and the world took to the streets to oppose the Iraq invasion; the global protests on February 15, 2003, may have been the largest global protest in human history. Sanders opposed the Iraq invasion—again, unlike many Democrats—along with Bush's other giveaways to corporations and attacks on civil liberties like the USA PATRIOT Act.

When he ran for Senate and won in 2007, Sanders took up issues similar to the ones he had in the House. He also fought to expand community health centers and defend the US Postal Service and Social Security from privatization and dismantlement. (He cofounded a Senate caucus called, fittingly, Defend Social Security.) He held public hearings on worker abuse and outright slavery in the tomato fields of Immokalee, Florida—hearings organized with the Coalition of Immokalee Workers, a labor rights organization for Florida farmworkers that first put on the map the issue of labor abuses in the state's tomato fields.

Sanders has a strong legislative record in Congress, but his fundamental goal has always been to shift the terms of public debate rather than hammering out compromises to pass legislation. "One of the most important roles I can play in Congress is to raise issues that, for a variety of reasons, other people choose not to deal with," he wrote in *Outsider in the White House*. "Just shifting the framework of debate can have enormous consequences."

Perhaps his most famous act as a senator came in opposition to the leader of the Democratic Party. In response to President Barack Obama's extensions of George W. Bush's tax cuts for the wealthy, on December 10, 2010, Sanders engaged in a nine-hour filibuster denouncing the tax cuts and the country's rampant inequality. "I'm not here to set any great records or to make a spectacle," he said at the speech's outset. "I am simply here today to take as long as I can to explain to the American people the fact that we have got to do a lot better than this agreement provides."

Progressives who were irate at Obama's willingness to extend such a massive giveaway to the rich were elated. On the evening of Sanders's filibuster, *Politico* reporter Shira Toeplitz wrote, "The left's been looking for a new hero. Tonight they latched onto one: Sen. Bernie Sanders." (In a sign of the kind of dismissive coverage of Sanders that the paper of record would later give his presidential campaigns, a *New York Times* reporter managed to write an entire article about the speech that noted Sanders jumped up and down at one point because his legs were cramping, and that he had oatmeal and coffee for breakfast beforehand, but said absolutely nothing about the actual political content of the speech.) The filibuster came less than a year before the Occupy Wall Street protests put economic inequality on the map in the United States. Sanders, as usual, was ahead of the curve.

Aside from the panoply of progressive policy measures Sanders fought for in the House, he also pioneered new ways to talk about major political issues. Sanders's foreign policy record has been imperfect: not only did he vote in favor of the Afghanistan invasion, but he has also hedged in the past on Israel's brutal occupation of Palestine (though his record is unquestionably one of the strongest on Palestine in Congress). But overall, his anti-imperialist instincts have been strong throughout his career, and they have only grown stronger in the last half-decade. He led the charge on invoking the

War Powers Resolution in March 2019 to stop US involvement in the Saudi war on Yemen, and took bolder progressive
foreign policy stances than any major presidential candidate
in recent history in his 2020 campaign (for example, denouncing military intervention in Iran and Venezuela, denouncing
the 2019 right-wing overthrow of democratically elected
Bolivian president Evo Morales as a "coup," and proposing
to leverage US aid to Israel in opposition to its occupation
of Palestine and abuses of Palestinians).

Sanders has also long fought to support veterans, especially
in the Veterans Administration. He became chair of the Senate
Veterans Committee in 2013, and has endeavored to stop
attempts to privatize the VA. "Some may see it as incongruous
for a strong progressive to be a fierce advocate for veterans'
rights. I don't, and never have," Sanders wrote in *Our Revolution*.
"I will continue to do everything that I can to make sure
the United States does not get entangled in wars that we
should not be fighting. But I will never blame the men and
women who do the fighting for getting us into those wars."

The soldiers on the front lines of America's imperialist
wars abroad, the ones who come home missing limbs and
with post-traumatic stress disorder, are often poor and people
of color. This is thanks in large part to the military's reliance
on economic conscription. In a country where social rights
such as health care and education are expensive and elusive,
the military attracts personnel with promises of social and
economic opportunities that should already be guaranteed.
Members of the armed forces report that these benefits are
the number-one reason they elected to join up. In his support
for rank-and-file soldiers while opposing war, perhaps
Sanders takes to heart that Eugene Debs line from the 1918
speech that landed him in jail: "The master class has always

declared the wars; the subject class has always fought the battles."

Sanders's strategy is far more likely to draw soldiers and veterans to join the antiwar cause, for which they are uniquely powerful spokespeople, than blanket anti-veteran sentiment on the Left. But it's also politically shrewd, in that it prevents the Right as well as liberals from scoring cheap points by attacking him as unpatriotic. The rhetoric of such attacks is jingoistic and absurd, used as a bludgeon against antiwar activists, but it can have emotional purchase, particularly in reactionary times when hawks are whipping up pro-war sentiment. Sanders's record of support for veterans prevents opponents from using that "anti-troop" canard against him when he agitates against war.

Sheer Force of Will

Without a unified mass movement to represent, Sanders marched to the beat of his own drum for decades. He stayed remarkably consistent in his politics during those years, seemingly through sheer force of will. All the incentives in US politics were for him to move rightward, to abandon his working-class politics following the trajectory of the Democratic Party, but he refused.

This should be a key lesson for current and aspiring leftist elected officials. In the long term, being consistent and steadfast in politics is not only morally correct, grounding politics in compassion for the working class and belief in ordinary people's right to live with dignity and security. It's also the *strategically savvy* thing to do. Objective political conditions change, and only those leaders whose principles remain unchanged can take full advantage of new openings and possibilities.

One central reason why so many people have flocked to Sanders's presidential campaigns is they respect and admire his political consistency over the years. The movements that helped spur Sanders to political action as a college student began dissipating around the time his political career began, but his refusal to abandon progressive demands—even at a time when the movements that had previously advanced them were weak—has paid off.

During his presidential campaigns, videos circulated widely on social media of Sanders repeating the same message about grotesque economic inequality in this country, from his time as mayor of Burlington to his tenure in the 1990s in the House to his time in the Senate to the presidential races. Voters find this consistency appealing. They trust him because of it. They see him as distinct from the politicians who embraced "ending welfare as we know it" when those policies were in vogue in the Democratic Party in the 1990s but back away from them now, or supported the 2003 invasion of Iraq but say they've now changed their minds, or who used to dismiss single-payer health care as a pipe dream but have suddenly begun considering it (or pretending to).

The clear lesson here is for leftist candidates to stick to their guns when it comes to progressive policies. Even if they pay a short-term political price for doing so, they'll gain the respect of ordinary people over time. Their perceived authenticity will help them make a convincing case that they represent an alternative and inspiring way of doing politics.

Much of Sanders's reliability owes to his own personal eccentricities. It takes an exceptionally strong-willed person, as well as one with raw political talent, to navigate the halls of power while purposefully rejecting all the entreaties and potential rewards of mainstream politics in favor of remaining

independent and committed to a left political project—
perhaps especially when that person is going it alone. There's
a reason Sanders called his book *Outsider in the White House*:
in his lifetime, there hasn't been anyone like him in American
politics, mostly because the organized movement of people
who think and act like Sanders has been in severe decline
since shortly after he became politically active.

But since Bernie first assumed political office, stagnating
wages and rising living costs have tested millions of people's
patience with the status quo and produced a political and
economic crisis that has finally begun to bring masses of
people around to his point of view. Things have reached a
boiling point in the new century. The 2008 financial crisis,
Occupy Wall Street, Black Lives Matter, labor uprisings in
Wisconsin in 2011, and the 2012 Chicago Teachers Union
strike further eroded popular tolerance for business as usual,
creating new openings for left-wing politics. Sanders was
personally willing and able to provide electoral leadership to
a movement getting back on its feet.

The unexpected popularity of Sanders's insurgent bids for
the presidency owed to both objective factors—worsening
material conditions, which formed the basis for a potential
resurgence of class consciousness—and subjective factors,
particularly his constancy and apparent authenticity, which
made him a natural leader for a country hungry for a break
from politics as usual. Sanders was the right guy in the right
place at the right time, but he also took advantage of that
confluence to make a profound impact on American political
culture.

Sanders's open identification as a democratic socialist gave
people a new vocabulary to match their evolving political
understanding. Most people who supported Sanders in the

2016 Democratic Party primary and plenty who didn't but warmed to him over the coming months and years became more amenable to the idea of socialism, loosely defined. It helped that Fox News and the right-wing establishment, resting on their laurels after the twentieth-century collapse of the Soviet Union, began to slander everything as "socialism" that didn't fit their aggressive conservative agenda, unwittingly inoculating millions of people and vacating the term of the ugly associations it had adopted during the Cold War era.

Luckily for those of us who are younger than Sanders, we don't have to endure the same isolation that he has throughout his career. There's a rising socialist movement in this country. And for the first time in decades, working people are no longer resigned to suffering passively. They are searching, listening, and increasingly they are fighting back. What that fight might look like in the decades to come is the subject of the rest of this book.

2

Class Struggle at the Ballot Box

The potential for socialists to use elections to spread our message and build our movement should be obvious to anyone paying attention. Sanders's 2016 presidential run showed that socialism actually had mainstream resonance. Two years later Alexandria Ocasio-Cortez, inspired by Bernie Sanders, ran for Congress and won, along with Rashida Tlaib and dozens of other democratic socialists at all levels of government. Without these and other successful national, state, and local campaigns around the country, we wouldn't have the rejuvenated Left that we have today.

Some socialists are uninterested in electoral politics, especially ones that have anything to do with the Democratic Party. The argument is that the party is a "graveyard" for the kinds of self-organized working-class movements we need to build in order to change the world, because the party isn't actually a workers' party—it's a party that has included organized labor, African Americans, feminists, environmentalists, and others with progressive ideas over the years, but those groups are stuck in an uncomfortable electoral alliance with capitalists. The Democratic Party is very adept at absorbing the energy from vibrant, disruptive working-class movements, bringing some of the leaders of those movements into the halls of power and conservatizing them, and completely squashing the transformative potential of organized challenges to the status quo.

These arguments aren't totally wrong. There are numerous possible pitfalls to using elections to change the world under capitalism, pitfalls that well-meaning socialists around the world have fallen into over the last century. And the Democratic Party *is* a fundamentally capitalist party, not a workers' party. In the long term, if we're going to win the kind of world we want, we'll need to ditch the Democrats and start a party of our own—one that isn't predicated on an alliance with the capitalist class.

But we can and should use elections to overcome the very real problems that detractors of electoral politics are identifying. Yes, the capitalist state is arranged against our project. And, yes, it is powerful—so powerful, in fact, that the only way to prevent annihilation at its hands is to give our movement a mass character that can fight the forces that seek to bury it.

Small groups of self-organized socialists and emboldened workers can play a very important role in changing the world. But without millions in our corner, we're no match for the United States' entrenched political machinery (not to mention its armies, police, and surveillance apparatuses). The only way we're going to build a durable movement to change the world is by building a very big movement to change the world. The socialist electoral campaigns that have played out over the last several years show us how we might go about solving this puzzle.

An Uneven Playing Field

We shouldn't have any illusions that the capitalist state will be easy to transform toward socialist ends. That's because the state isn't neutral territory: under capitalism, the state is fundamentally biased toward capitalists and pro-capitalist policies. For one thing, elected politicians and unelected high-ranking officeholders in government are often capitalists or beneficiaries of the capitalist order themselves. The average member of Congress, for example, is worth over a million dollars. More importantly, because capitalists have power over the means of production, they have power over what average people need in order to survive—and that power bleeds over into the electoral sphere, where capitalists have an outsized and undemocratic ability to influence what elected officials do and don't do, and shape political outcomes.

Under capitalism, the only thing worse than being exploited and abused by your boss is *not* being exploited and abused by your boss, because that means you don't have a job and thus can't support yourself and your family. And just as capitalists can fire workers and leave them without the means to survive, capitalists can also withdraw their investments from entire regions or countries, leaving those countries high and dry without jobs and income. This is what's called capital flight, or in its most retaliatory form, a "capital strike." Workers can strike by withholding their labor, but capital can also strike by pulling investments.

Because the vast majority of us are dependent on those investments, capitalists have us over a barrel. They can punish governments that enact policies they don't like, for whatever reason. Did a pro-worker government pass high taxes on corporations to fund social welfare programs, or tell a factory owner to pay workers higher wages and stop poisoning the air and water with noxious emissions? Those corporations can simply pull their investments from that city, state, or country. Capitalists can always take their ball and go play somewhere else; workers and governments can't.

The result for that government will then almost certainly be a crisis, because without those investments, workers who worked for that corporation could lose their jobs, all the secondary economic markets that were stimulated by that company's investments will suffer, and the government will lose much-needed tax revenue from those investments. It's a trump card that capitalists can play against governments whose policies aren't to their liking. It's not insurmountable— leftist governments have options open to them like capital controls, which can prevent capitalists from pulling their money out of a given territory. But it makes life for any left party trying to antagonize capitalists very, very tough.

Because of these structural constraints, we can't simply vote the new world into being. However, socialists can engage in electoral politics in a way that democratically builds the working class's capacity for self-organization. There are status quo electoral politics—in which social change is entrusted exclusively to elected politicians, left to their own devices after victory—and then there are class-struggle electoral politics.

Class-Struggle Electoral Politics

Class-struggle electoral politics are about using elections to popularize socialist ideas, clarify class lines, energize people to fight on their own, and build movements beyond elections. Running class-struggle electoral campaigns is about empowering the working-class movements that are necessary to remake society.

There's usually little point in running for office if you're not trying to win—especially now, when socialist ideas are popular and winning is a real possibility. But class-struggle electoral politics aim to use elections to do three things *beyond* simply trying to win: raise the expectations of ordinary working people, unite them against a common capitalist enemy, and promote mass working-class movements outside the state.

A class-struggle politician is someone who refuses to accept prevailing ideas about society and insists that a different world is actually possible. All people deserve a good education, a safe and comfortable home, quality health care, clean air and water, and free time to enjoy their lives. But in our society, these things are often luxuries enjoyed only by the rich. Most politicians tell working-class people that it's impossible for the government to provide these things in full to all people, but that fortunately we can look to the market to fill the gaps. Even those who claim to be sympathetic to achieving a better world often argue that the resources just aren't there, even as the wealthy make record profits and get huge tax breaks.

Others pay lip service to much-needed reforms as good ideas but claim they are politically impossible, without even fighting for them. This group, to which many liberal American politicians today belong, might say they support some social welfare programs. But they typically insist on complicated, divisive, and often degrading means testing to ensure that only those who "deserve" the benefits get them—all for programs that are woefully insufficient even for those who do receive the benefits. They write off universal social programs as a fantasy. Rahm Emanuel, the Democratic former Chicago mayor and chief of staff for presidents Clinton and Obama who champions the party's pro-corporate, rightward turn every opportunity he gets, wrote in an October 2019 op-ed against Medicare for All, "Our approach to health care needs to be centered on political reality, not a pipe dream." After the 2016 election, Hillary Clinton famously denigrated Bernie Sanders's argument for Medicare for All or free college tuition for all as akin to a promise of giving every American a pony.

With so many politicians dismissing transformative political change in this way, it's no surprise that many working-class people are resigned to a diminished quality of life. A class-struggle politician aims to turn that resignation into hope and determination. This is what we mean by "raising the expectations of the working class."

A good example of this in recent decades is the fight for single-payer health care. When Sanders first introduced his version of a single-payer bill to Congress in 1993, he said, "The American people believe that health care must be a right of all citizens and not just the privilege of the wealthy." He supported the policy before introducing the bill and has supported it since, throughout entire decades during which it was written off as a fantasy. On the campaign trail in 2016, he used his massive platform to convince people that working-class Americans deserve Medicare for All, and that it is completely politically possible to achieve it, as long as ordinary people and politicians alike are prepared to fight for it.

We haven't won Medicare for All yet, but as overwhelming numbers of Americans now support it—recent polls have regularly found that majorities of people and even occasional majorities of *Republicans* back a universal public health insurance program—Sanders's approach has been vindicated.

There's no better personal example of this transformation in action than the rise of Alexandria Ocasio-Cortez, the millennial socialist who seemingly out of nowhere won a race for the House of Representatives in 2018. At an October 2019 Sanders rally in Queens, New York, in front of twenty-six thousand people gathered on a sunny day in front of the East River, the Manhattan skyline in the background, Ocasio-Cortez told a story:

> Last February I was working as a waitress in downtown Manhattan ... I didn't have health care, I wasn't being paid a living wage, and I didn't think that I deserved any of those things. Because that is the script that we tell working people here and all over this country, that your inherent worth and value as a human being is dependent on an income that another person decided to underpay us. But what we're here to do is to turn around that very basic logic.
>
> It wasn't until I heard of a man by the name of Bernie Sanders that I began to question and assert and recognize my inherent value as a human being that deserves health care, housing, education, and a living wage.

Sanders did not wait until the idea for Medicare for All had been fully poll-tested and trial-ballooned before beginning to agitate for it. Instead, he stepped out ahead of the populace. He made demands that were ambitious and struck a chord with people and spoke to their suffering—spoke to, for example, the hardship of underpaid young workers like Ocasio-Cortez. In the process, he expanded the horizon of people's political imaginations.

Still, it's not enough to make ambitious demands. A class-struggle politician also has to explain why those demands haven't been met, focusing on the obstacles thrown up by the ruling class and on the underlying dynamics of capitalism that empower the wealthy few. They must use every opportunity they can to tell a new story about society, one that offers an explanation for why so many people suffer while a select few enjoy their lives in relative comfort. This new story has an antagonist and a protagonist: the bad guy is the tiny capitalist class, and the good guy is the huge and diverse working class.

For a class-struggle politician, the adversary does not go unnamed. As one corporate lobbyist complained in May 2019 in the *New York Times*, "To a hammer, everything is a nail. And to Sanders, everything is an issue created by millionaires and billionaires." This clarifying and polarizing message is a very good thing indeed—both because it happens to be true (the rich have incredible control over our lives and everything that transpires on our planet, and are the ones responsible for most of our worst ills), and because it's extremely effective political communication.

Politicians from both major parties routinely issue vague calls for unity and harmony. But class-struggle politicians know that class conflict will never disappear under capitalism—it's inherent to it. The only question is whether the working class will succeed in fighting back. So they don't paper over conflict. They call instead for a specific type of unity: that of the working class in struggle against a common enemy.

Among the working class, class-struggle politicians urge solidarity across lines of difference. Bernie Sanders explained this in a speech at that same October 2019 rally, when he asked the 26,000 in attendance to look around them and identify someone who seemed different from themselves. "Are you willing to fight for that person who you don't even know as much as you're willing to fight for yourself?" he asked. "Are you willing to fight for young people drowning in student debt even if you are not? Are you willing to fight to ensure that every American has health care as a human right even if you have good health care? Are you willing to fight for frightened immigrant neighbors even if you are native born?"

Finally, a class-struggle politician is someone who understands that the only way to actually make lasting change is to build and harness the power of working people outside the state. They know that even when they're in office, they will be up against the formidable power of the capitalist class. To truly transform society, they understand that they need huge numbers of ordinary people to build mass movements that can exert pressure of their own.

As Sanders put it in an October 2019 interview with CNBC's John Harwood:

BERNIE SANDERS: Right now you have a Congress and a White House that are dominated by a corporate elite who have unbelievable amounts of money and influence over the political and economic life of this country. I'm not going to be dominated by those guys. I will take them on and I'll beat them.

The way we beat them is with the understanding that real change has never taken place without millions of people standing up and demanding that change. That is the history of the labor movement, the civil rights movement, the women's movement, the gay movement, the environmental movement. I will not only be commander in chief of the military, I will be organizer in chief. I will be organizing with a strong grassroots movement.

We already have the nucleus. It'll be involving the labor unions, the African American communities, the Latino community, the young people of this country. All people who believe in justice, working-class people, who are prepared to stand up and fight and take on the corporate elite . . .

JOHN HARWOOD: But even if you get elected, even if it's successful to the point that Democrats win a small majority in the Senate, is [conservative Democrat and West Virginia senator] Joe Manchin going to vote for your program? Is [conservative Democrat and Montana senator] Jon Tester going to vote for your program?

BERNIE SANDERS: Yeah. Damn right they will. You know why? We're going to go to West Virginia.

Your average politician sits around and he or she thinks, "Let's see. If I do this, I'm going to have the big money interests putting 30-second ads against me. So I'd better not do it." But now they're going to have to think, "If I don't support an agenda that works for working people, I'm going to have President Sanders coming to my state and rallying working-class people."

You know what? The 1 percent is very powerful—no denying that. The 99%, when they're organized and prepared to stand up and fight, they are far more powerful.

Bernie Sanders has been exemplary on this front not just in word, but in deed. His campaign in 2016 was unconventional in many respects, but it was what he did afterward that showed the extent to which he believes in using electoral politics, as both a candidate and office-holder, to build movements of the working class outside the state.

Organizer in Chief

Sanders told John Harwood that if he won, he would be the "organizer in chief." No president has ever articulated their role this way—not even President Barack Obama, who was himself a former community organizer. What would being an "organizer in chief" look like? What Sanders did after losing the 2016 Democratic primary to Clinton gives us a good idea.

Naming and Shaming

Sanders has both personally gone after major corporations and wealthy CEOs, and used his campaign machinery to support striking workers and other protests. For example, in June 2018, Sanders took the stage at a rally attended by hundreds of Disneyland workers in Anaheim, California. "I want to hear the moral defense of a company that makes $9 billion in profits, $400 million for their CEOs and have a 30-year worker going hungry," he said. "Tell me how that is right." He added, "The struggle that you are waging here in Anaheim is not just for you. It is a struggle for millions of workers all across this country who are sick and tired of working longer hours for lower wages."

The union that represents the workers, UNITE HERE, was at that point in contract negotiations with Disney. Sanders chose to use his platform to help them win their contract fight. A few days later, he wrote an op-ed for the *Guardian* in which he publicized the workers' testimonies he had heard in Anaheim and wrote,

> What these workers are doing, standing up against the greed of one of the most powerful and profitable

corporations in America, takes an enormous amount of courage. If they are able to win a livable wage with good benefits from Disney, it will be a shot heard around the world. It will give other low-wage workers at profitable corporations throughout the country the strength they need to demand a living wage with good benefits.

The next month, Disney agreed to pay its unionized workers at Disneyland a minimum of $15 an hour; in August, it followed suit at Disney World in Florida. Sanders didn't create the fight at Disney himself, of course—workers there were already unionized and fighting for better pay and working conditions. But he used his massive bully pulpit to support these workers, in a way that went far beyond the typical photo ops that Democratic candidates pause for on picket lines and at union conventions during campaign season.

Then, in late August, he blasted Disney for securing large tax breaks for itself while many of its workers were still paid so little. After that, Sanders generalized the fight by introducing legislation in November to raise the federal minimum wage to $15 an hour—a change that would affect 40 million people, or 25 percent of the workforce.

In April 2018, Sanders also publicly criticized Amazon, saying, "You know what Amazon paid in federal income taxes last year? Zero." In May, he posted a video online taking aim at the company, stating that "[Jeff] Bezos makes more in 10 seconds than the median Amazon employee makes in a year: $28,466." The company, which rarely issues public comments in response to controversy, called Sanders's attacks "inaccurate and misleading" and invited Sanders to tour one of its warehouses. Sanders accepted the invitation, but added publicly: "I remain deeply concerned about Amazon, an enormously profitable corporation, paying workers wages that are so low that they are forced to depend on federal programs like Medicaid, food stamps and public housing for survival. At a time of exploding profits, I would hope that Amazon would pay everyone who works in your fulfillment centers a living wage."

Sanders continued to speak out against Bezos and Amazon throughout the summer, including hosting a town hall in July—titled "CEOs vs. Workers"—where he screened a video about Bezos's personal wealth, the greatest in the world. In August, Sanders spoke out against Amazon yet again, and circulated a petition among his supporters calling for Amazon to increase pay and improve working conditions.

Under intense public scrutiny because of Sanders's agitation, Amazon quietly began offering workers $50 gift cards to post on social media about how much they enjoyed working in its warehouses. Sanders found out about the scheme, and publicly embarrassed Amazon by creating a video lambasting the company's attempts at spin. The video ended with Sanders calling on Amazon to pay its warehouse workers $15 an hour.

In September, Sanders submitted a piece of legislation to the Senate that would tax large companies for every dollar spent on social services used by their low-wage workers. Workers rely on those programs to make ends meet in the absence of pay high enough to cover their living costs, and the public foots the bill when it should be the companies instead. Sanders called the bill the "Stop BEZOS Act." Bezos's name was transformed into an acronym that stands for "Bad Employers by Zeroing Out Subsidies."

It's worth pausing on this point for a moment: a sitting US senator introduced a bill that targeted the world's richest man in its very name. Sanders essentially said, *Here is a very rich man. This man's name is Jeff Bezos. Bezos is going about his business, doing his rich man thing, taking untold billions that he never toiled to earn.* The title of the proposed legislation communicated a clear message: *We need to stop Jeff Bezos from doing this.*

(Sanders has a flair for naming and shaming the rich and powerful. In 2019 when he faced criticism from JPMorgan Chase chairman and CEO Jamie Dimon, Sanders responded on social media, "Jamie Dimon is the billionaire CEO of a Wall Street bank that was fined $13 billion for mortgage fraud, admitted to wrongly foreclosing on military officials, paid a settlement for bribing foreign officials and received a $416 billion taxpayer bailout from the Federal Reserve and the Treasury Department." He added sarcastically, "Jamie. Thanks so much for your advice.")

The Stop BEZOS Act went nowhere in the Republican-controlled Senate, but the purpose of the bill was twofold: to model legislation that ought to pass under more favorable political conditions, and to pressure Bezos into caving. Sanders was successful. In October, Amazon announced that its warehouse workers would be paid a minimum of $15 an hour.

News soon broke that what Bezos had given with the one hand, he had taken away with the other, raising the company's minimum wage but taking away stock options and incentive pay for some workers in the process. The raise wasn't perfect. But Sanders had taken a demand that came from years of organizing and striking by fast-food and retail workers—the demand for $15 an hour—and used it to shame the world's richest man. That shaming caused the notoriously unflinching Bezos to flinch.

As with Disney, Sanders hasn't backed off Amazon. He turned his attention from pay to benefits and working conditions, saying that we "must recognize that workers' rights don't stop at the minimum wage." In early presidential campaign speeches, Sanders frequently told large crowds that Amazon paid nothing in federal income taxes, a fact that was met with jeers. In June 2019, he criticized Amazon for offering a high-interest consumer credit card—a practice Sanders has said he would outlaw—and on another occasion accused Amazon of contributing to the homelessness crisis in Seattle when it used its muscle to kill an important tax introduced by socialist city council member Kshama Sawant to build affordable housing in the city.

Sanders followed up his Stop BEZOS Act with a Stop WALMART Act in November 2018, which according to CNN would "prevent large companies from buying back stock unless they pay all employees at least $15 an hour, allow workers to earn up to seven days of paid sick leave and limit CEO compensation to no more than 150 times the median pay of all staffers." He began publicly agitating against Walmart, calling the company's greed "grotesque" and "absurd."

Sanders posted to social media a video of himself in 1995 railing against Walmart, saying, "People should know that the reason that the rich get richer, that our jobs are going to Mexico, that corporations are downsizing, is that the major corporations, Walmart among many others, have tremendous sway over the political process." He said about the old video, "It's as true today as it was in 1995: We have a rigged economy that allows corporations like Walmart to have an outsized influence on American politics. It's time to stand up and demand a country and economy that works for all of us, not just a few."

(Sanders has been saying the same things for decades. In 2019 he posted to social media: "My skeptics often accuse me of being boring, of hammering the same themes. They're probably right. It's never made sense to me that a few people have incredible wealth and power while most have none. Should we ever achieve justice, I promise I'll write some new speeches.")

He began a social media crusade against Walmart that extended into the next year when, in June 2019, he was invited by Walmart workers, who had long been organizing at the company, to crash the company's annual stockholder convention. On the convention grounds in Bentonville, Arkansas, Peter Frampton played a concert to Walmart shareholders, but off campus Sanders spoke to Walmart workers, telling them,

> This company, owned by the wealthiest family in America, can pay $15 an hour. Today we are here to fight for the dignity of Walmart employees, to make sure that every employee at Walmart has at least a living wage . . . The entire country is watching. The country is so tired of this massive level of income and wealth inequality, where the people on top make billions and billions and working people struggle.

Sanders purchased a single share of Walmart stock in 1994 (so he could, in his words, "keep an eye on the company") which allowed him to attend the convention and submit a shareholder resolution. He chose to submit a proposal as a proxy for a Walmart employee who was not allowed into the convention. It was a poetic metaphor for Bernie Sanders's role in American politics—on the inside, largely alone, representing those outside.

His proposal called for allowing workers to sit on Walmart's board, which he said in an interview is "enormously important because at the end of the day, working people have got to have some control over how they spend at least eight hours a day." The proposal was killed, but Sanders turned his social media accounts over to the Walmart workers for the duration of the weekend.

There are too many examples of Sanders's anticorporate agitation to list here. The point is that Sanders has, alongside organizing workers, used his enormous profile to attack some of the most abusive and wealthiest corporations in the world, in a far more creative and sustained way than we've ever seen from Democratic politicians. In the process, he's proven that those corporations can be humbled—an example that average workers around the country need to see and believe if they're going to summon the courage to fight their own bosses.

To the Picket Line!

In his 2020 campaign, Sanders went a step further, doing something unprecedented in the history of American presidential politics: he leveraged his campaign data infrastructure to bolster rallies and picket lines in cities and towns throughout the country, using his campaign lists to turn out support for workers at McDonald's, Amazon, Wabtec, Delta Airlines, Nissan, Disney, General Motors, the University of California, the University of Illinois, the University of Chicago; teachers in Los Angeles and West Virginia; and more. His communications often included specific information about where and when to meet. This wasn't just a vague gesture in support of organizing workers—the campaign was turning its supporters out to real-life protest action and communicating that if you like Sanders's message on the campaign trail, you should also be out in the streets supporting strikes and protests.

When Los Angeles teachers went on strike in January 2019, Sanders directed supporters to donate to the strike fund. Over $100,000 was raised. When University of California workers went on a one-day strike, the Sanders campaign directed supporters near campuses to the picket lines, and reported that one thousand "responded with interest or committed to go to a protest" in support.

"This is a workers' movement as much as it's a presidential campaign," Sanders staffer Bill Neidhardt told the progressive magazine *In These Times*. "And that's exactly how we want it to be. That's how you win. With a movement."

Even when engaging in the typical duties of Democratic campaigning, Sanders hasn't stuck to the script. He kicked off a Chicago rally in March 2019, for example, with Destiny Harris, an eighteen-year-old black activist with the #NoCopAcademy campaign, a black youth–led effort to stop construction of a $95 million law enforcement training center on Chicago's West Side. Activists argued that the city already spends far too much on police—who then often end up brutalizing or killing black youth—and should spend that money on youth and community services instead.

"I did not know economic development looked like more investment in jails, policing, and mass incarceration," Harris said in response to the justification that the city's political leaders gave for the project.

But the project was strongly backed by then mayor Rahm Emanuel and the rest of the city's political class. The pro–law enforcement arguments were so loud that opposition from elected leaders became nearly unthinkable in Chicago. When city council member and Democratic Socialists of America member Carlos Ramirez-Rosa became one of the lone voices to speak up against it, he was expelled from the council's

Latino Caucus and treated as a political pariah in the city. No local elected officials would touch the #NoCopAcademy campaign—yet Bernie chose a #NoCopAcademy activist to open up his rally, exposing his entire audience to the movement's demands and political reasoning.

Months later, in September 2019, when the Chicago Teachers Union was preparing to strike, Sanders left the campaign trail in Iowa to join the union for a rally. Democratic presidential candidates joining striking workers isn't out of the ordinary; what *was* out of the ordinary was that Sanders basically abandoned his stump speech and, instead of giving vague platitudes about supporting the union, spoke directly to its contract demands, against a mayor, Lori Lightfoot, who stonewalled the union and eventually pushed it into a strike.

Sanders has also used his email lists to warn immigrants—a particularly vulnerable section of the working class—about impending raids by Immigration and Customs Enforcement (ICE). These emails have listed specific cities that are set to be targeted by the agency, and contained "Know Your Rights" information in English and Spanish. This move was intimately connected to his labor movement support strategy: an ICE-targeted immigrant population constitutes a broken link in the chain of working-class solidarity. In addition to being immoral and oppressive on its own grounds, the stripping of immigrants' political rights makes them hypervulnerable to exploitation, which undercuts the efforts of all workers, regardless of their immigration status, to organize as a bloc for higher pay and better working and living conditions for all.

Sanders's use of his campaign data to protect immigrant workers and drive protest and picket turnout is the most concrete example of Sanders treating his campaign as an opportunity to materially build and strengthen the labor movement. In the United States, we've never seen anything like it before. *Politico* reporter Holly Otterbein wrote in August 2019 (before the campaign had kicked into high gear) that

> Sanders' campaign said it has sent hundreds of thousands of emails and a half-million texts to his supporters to push them to attend more than 50 strikes, protests and other events this year. It's a significant investment for a presidential campaign, considering there's only so much time or money Sanders' supporters are willing to give overall, and he's asking that they commit themselves to causes that only indirectly benefit his candidacy.

The strategy shows the degree to which Sanders still believes what he believed in 1977, when he left the Liberty Union Party on account of its narrow focus on elections. The purpose of electoral politics isn't simply to maneuver to win votes, he said then—it is "to create a situation in which the ordinary working people take what rightfully belongs to them." That is the maxim at the heart of class-struggle electoral politics.

Contesting for State Power

To raise expectations, polarize along class lines, and build working-class movements on a scale large enough to have a real impact, socialists have to aim high and be willing to run oppositional, insurgent campaigns against established politicians. Contesting for state power in order to build class struggle is only possible when we take on political power players who have convinced everyone, even socialists, of their endurance and imperviousness.

Many people have been inspired by Sanders to give it a shot. One of these, as we have already mentioned, was Alexandria Ocasio-Cortez.

When Ocasio-Cortez, then a bartender, decided to run for Congress against powerful Democratic Party incumbent Joe Crowley, it seemed like a longshot. Crowley had served as the congressional representative of New York's 14th District, covering parts of Queens and the Bronx, since 1999. In that time, he had done little for the working-class residents of his district, soaking up real estate money while the city gentrified and its residents were financially squeezed and increasingly displaced. But he climbed the party ladder, becoming chair of the House Democratic Caucus in 2017. He was rumored to be the chosen successor to Nancy Pelosi for the top Democrat in the House of Representatives.

During Ocasio-Cortez's race, Crowley was living full-time in Virginia, not New York. Ocasio-Cortez identified this as his weak spot: he was out of touch with people on the ground. To beat him, she campaigned hard. When she won, she posted a picture of her worn-out sneakers on social media. "I knocked doors until rainwater came through my soles," she said.

Early in the race, Ocasio-Cortez invited Crowley to debate her at a community center. Unconcerned about her challenge, he declined, sending a surrogate instead. Ocasio-Cortez went forward with the debate, condemning Crowley's absenteeism and telling the crowd, "For so long, we haven't had these forums. The only reason we are here is because we organized for the first primary election in fourteen years." When the faux debate ended, Ocasio-Cortez stayed behind to talk to

African and Yemeni immigrant constituents about their néeds and her plans. Crowley's surrogate was nowhere in sight.

This was the race in a microcosm: while Crowley had money and influence in abundance, he lacked basic organizing skills or any interest in cultivating them, relying instead on professional connections and donations to grease the wheels. With intense canvassing, genuine community engagement, and a message of economic equality and social justice, a young working-class woman from the Bronx could take on one of the most powerful Democrats in Washington and win. As Ocasio-Cortez herself was fond of saying during the race, "We meet a machine with a movement."

Since her victory over Crowley, Ocasio-Cortez has become one of the most high-profile figures in American politics, with an audience far exceeding that of a typical congressional freshman. On the right, her insistence on calling herself a democratic socialist has made her an object of fear and ridicule (which, rather than hurting her, seems to only strengthen her). In the Democratic Party, she's quietly regarded as a threat to the party power structure who is likely to inspire imitators. While Democratic politicians are occasionally happy to be seen agreeing with the celebrity congresswoman, behind the scenes, the Democratic Party gatekeepers have done every-thing they can to kneecap challengers like her.

In 2019, the Democratic Congressional Campaign Committee introduced new rules intended to hamstring left insurgents like Ocasio-Cortez. The group, one of the few visible bureaucratic apparatuses of the Democratic Party, announced that it would no longer give any work to consul-tants, pollsters, and other political professionals who lend their efforts to progressive and democratic socialist candidates seek-ing to depose Democratic Party incumbents. Ocasio-Cortez was fighting the Democratic Party power brokers; now they were fighting back.

One of the most important effects of Ocasio-Cortez's victory has been to undermine the impression that the Democratic Party establishment is undefeatable. Even when the party wins at the ballot box, it is far from beloved. Its continued success relies on widespread popular resignation, a false sense of political immutability, and the absence of an alternative political strategy to win policies that benefit the many.

But in certain places, the Democratic Party's foundation is shakier than we think—especially, it seems, in urban blue districts where the party establishment is still steeped in old-school machine politics and slow to react to changes on the ground, while under its nose gentrification and rising living costs have eroded support for the status quo.

"The entire New York political establishment, they have no idea what's going on," Ocasio-Cortez said at a Democratic Socialists of America event during her campaign. "This race is winnable. And don't let anyone tell you any different, because the power out there, I'm telling you, is an illusion." A primary task of class-struggle electoral politics is to expose that illusion.

Since joining Congress, Ocasio-Cortez has continued to raise the profile of democratic socialism and raise the expectations of the working class. But for the first nine months of her tenure in Congress, we held our breath.

She was being pulled in a million different directions, and as heartened as we were to see her fight the Democratic Party establishment, at other times we feared she would be co-opted—not because she was personally untrustworthy, but because history is littered with examples of young, energetic progressives who crusade against the political system, only to be fully absorbed by that system, their combativeness toned down, and the hope they once represented extinguished.

In September 2019, the *New York Times* published a story that portrayed her as a politician already learning that she'll catch more flies with honey than vinegar. "Ms. Ocasio-Cortez has tempered her brash, institution-be-damned style with something different: a careful political calculus that adheres more closely to the unwritten rules of Washington she once disdained," the article read.

Ocasio-Cortez bristled at the portrayal. On Twitter she wrote, "There will always be powerful interest in promoting the idea that the left is losing power 1 way or another. The big way they try to dismantle the left isn't to attack it, but to gaslight & deflate it." She accused the article of "dripping condescension." This is the centrist playbook: demoralize and diminish the Left by declaring the battle over already.

It was unfair for the mainstream press to dub Ocasio-Cortez another would-be reformer who had capitulated to the conservatizing pressures of the Democratic Party establishment. She continually challenged the neoliberal status quo, especially in the realm of policy. Her Green New Deal legislation is phenomenally ambitious, as is her new suite of anti-poverty bills called "A Just Society." Still, socialists were on pins and needles. There was a litmus test coming up, one that would tell us more than anything to date whether Ocasio-Cortez was bending the knee or standing strong: Would she endorse Bernie Sanders?

She could have endorsed Elizabeth Warren, more conservative than Sanders but not entirely lacking in progressive bona fides, and much more palatable to the Democratic Party establishment. Or she could have declined to endorse anyone.

Or she could have opted for a dual endorsement of Warren and Sanders.

Endorsing Sanders would further alienate Ocasio-Cortez from the Democratic Party establishment who, beholden to corporate interests, were uniformly hostile to Sanders's campaigns. It also might lead to Ocasio-Cortez being shut out of important decisions in the party, being denied leadership positions, or possibly even being primaried by her own party. Remaining neutral in the primary could have allowed Ocasio-Cortez to avoid unnecessary heat from the party, giving her room to more easily maneuver in Congress. That would have been the careerist move, setting herself up to occupy a progressive lane within the party, but demonstrating that she was willing to tone down her politics enough to play nice with the party's power brokers.

But in October, she decided against all that. She endorsed Bernie Sanders.

The inside story of the endorsement as reported by *Politico* was dramatic stuff, the part of the Sanders Hollywood biopic where the string music swells. As he was lying in a Las Vegas hospital bed after a heart attack in October 2019, Ocasio-Cortez called him. Despite his suffering a setback that threatened to derail his campaign, Ocasio-Cortez didn't even wait until Sanders left the hospital: she pledged her support to him.

"Think about the courage of this person [Ocasio-Cortez] who says, 'You know, I know what you just went through but I have so much trust and confidence in you that you are the one who will fight the fight that I believe in. I'm with you,'" Sanders's 2020 campaign manager Faiz Shakir said.

That endorsement was a clear sign by Ocasio-Cortez that she would not take the path of least resistance in her political career—that she was willing to not only fight for progressive social change, but do so alongside a candidate who had antagonized the Democratic Party for nearly four decades.

Ocasio-Cortez was joined by congressional freshmen Rashida Tlaib and Ilhan Omar. The three women breathed new life into his campaign. And they showed that Sanders was not alone—he indeed represented a movement, and they were willing to stick their necks out and provide electoral leadership to that movement for years to come.

By endorsing Sanders, Ocasio-Cortez, Tlaib, and Omar surely angered some colleagues and jeopardized some relationships in the short run. But there's no avoiding that if you're going to be a champion for the working class. Any attempt to stay in the good graces of the establishment while also building a movement against it won't work. Best to signal that you've chosen your side early on, then work with others as best you can but with the clear understanding that your principles won't be compromised.

That's how Sanders did it. And it seemed that Ocasio-Cortez, inspired from the outset by Bernie Sanders, had decided to continue emulating him. In an interview with CBS about her endorsement, she said: "Understanding the pressures there are on the inside to conform, and to have seen them and experienced them firsthand, it's astounded me frankly that [Sanders] has been there fighting for me long before I got to the halls of Congress, and fighting for people like me."

At that rally in Queens, Ocasio-Cortez elaborated on the nature of that congressional pressure:

> The halls of Congress are no joke. It is no joke. Standing up to corporate power, and established interests is no joke.

It's not just about standing up and saying these things, but behind closed doors, your arm is twisted, the vise pressure of political pressure gets put on you, every trick in the book, psychological, and otherwise is to get us to abandon the working class.

Rather than tempering or taming her, Ocasio-Cortez's experiences being wooed and manipulated by the Democratic Party establishment actually made her *more* committed to standing her ground, not less.

Democratic socialists and other progressives in the Sanders coalition breathed a sigh of relief. Far from a flash-in-the-pan progressive trend, it seemed we now had multiple electoral anchors of a broader left movement in this country. They proved they were unafraid to buck the Democratic Party establishment—that they had their sights set not just on the next session of Congress or the next election, but on a future for working-class politics.

The Rise of DSA

One of the most important developments after Sanders's 2016 campaign and Trump's victory was the emergence onto the national scene of the Democratic Socialists of America (DSA). Sanders isn't a member of the organization, but Ocasio-Cortez is, along with Tlaib. DSA played an important role as part of a broader progressive coalition working to get Ocasio-Cortez elected, and is leading the way in socialist electoral organizing. The rise of DSA is one of the most inspiring developments in the political landscape since 2016—and as members of the organization who are intimately familiar with its trajectory, we believe that rise is only just beginning.

DSA was formed in 1982 from a merger of two existing socialist groups, the New American Movement and the Democratic Socialist Organizing Committee, and was originally led by Michael Harrington, the most high-profile American socialist of that era. Before 2016, DSA was a relatively small socialist group, and one that leaned much further to the right than it does now on a number of key issues: it was tepid in its support of Palestinian liberation from Israel, for example, and often supported Democratic candidates of any stripe over Republicans rather than withhold its endorsement in the absence of socialist politics.

But DSA also had a noble tradition of opposition to Stalinism and robust internal democracy. The group kept the socialist torch alight during dark times for the American Left, and did so in a nonsectarian way. While its membership idled for years before the Sanders campaign, and few on the Left saw it as a dynamic and exciting organization, DSA was one of the only major socialist organizations in America that came out in strong support of Sanders in 2016, and was the only socialist organization whose outward-facing orientation and "big-tent" approach to multiple strands of left-wing ideology made it a suitable home for thousands of new socialist activists.

After Sanders's first presidential campaign, DSA was completely reborn, and its activities in the electoral sphere continue to generate new opportunities for socialist organizing. Its membership increased by 25 percent during the lead-up to the general election. When Trump won, DSA saw an additional 30 percent increase nearly overnight. As we write this book in late 2019, national membership is approaching 60,000.

While these new socialist recruits represent a small number of the people whose political outlooks were transformed by

Sanders's candidacy, they now constitute the majority of the organized socialist Left in the United States. Today, all but a handful of Americans who are members of any socialist group are members of DSA. This is in large part because DSA backed Sanders from the beginning. Many other socialist organizations held Sanders at arm's length because he ran on the Democratic Party ballot line, and such groups are opposed to any campaigns within the party on principle.

The growth is also attributable to the fact that DSA has a low barrier to entry. It's easy and cheap (even free, if you don't have the money) to sign up to become a member, and it's fine to make a minimal commitment to action as a dues-paying member. But the group has plenty of opportunities for action and political education upon recruitment. Its big-tent orientation welcomes socialists of all stripes and does not impose a strict and single ideological line, though different political tendencies democratically make the case for certain kinds of politics or campaigns over others.

After the election of Donald Trump, waves of mass protest rocked the nation. His inauguration was greeted with unrest in the streets of Washington, DC. Shortly thereafter, we saw the Women's March in opposition to his blatant misogyny, and enormous protests against his proposed Muslim ban that shut down major airports throughout the country. A new consensus was emerging left of center: to sit idly by was to be complicit in the coming atrocities of the Trump administration. That consensus was and is much larger than socialism and DSA. But DSA strongly benefited from it, and the new socialists who joined were ready to get their hands dirty.

Nick Conder of Louisville, Kentucky, who is twenty-eight, joined before Trump won. "I had been aware of DSA for a couple years at that point but didn't join because I felt like socialist organizations only really existed in larger cities than where I lived in Kentucky," he says. "Bernie Sanders's first campaign made me rethink things. I saw everybody I know starting to identify as socialists for the first time and realized we could organize even here. DSA had been active in supporting Bernie before he even had started running, so I felt like it was the most serious organization to be a part of and help build."

Kristin Schall of New York City, who is thirty-five, joined DSA at 10 p.m. on the night of the 2016 election. "It had become clear that Trump was going to win and I knew that I had to get involved in building something," she says. "I joined DSA because no other organization felt right. Having experienced the Left for quite a few years, I already knew the landscape. But the people I was meeting who were joining DSA weren't what I had previously expected from the organization. They were younger and more radical, and several people who I trusted had joined. So I decided to make the leap and go for it."

"I had never been involved in politics in any way until I joined DSA the day after Trump was elected," says Aaron Taube of New York City, aged thirty. Taube graduated college in 2011, in the middle of the Great Recession. "It was bleak," he says. Initially hoping to become a sports journalist but disillusioned by a brutal job market and a string of crappy internships, he took a job as a researcher at a news service for corporate attorneys, Law360—an "exploitative, miserable workplace."

Between the conditions at work, what he learned on the job about how the US legal system is stacked against workers, and later seeing his own former coworkers try to unionize only to face massive resistance from their bosses, he felt he was "watching the gears of capital work to protect the share-holders from the workers having power. I saw the class struggle up close." He watched Bernie's campaign with interest and donated, but didn't get involved beyond that. Then Trump won. The reactionary forces he unleashed included antisem-itism, which personally worried Taube, who is Jewish. And all illusions about the Democrats disappeared.

"I was like, 'Oh, actually, the people in charge are totally incompetent.' It's not even so much that neoliberalism is bad— these people [Democrats] can't even win. The world is on fire, and the Democrats are just not up to the task of fixing it." Sanders and DSA seemed to offer an alternative. "Bernie Sanders's campaign continued that process and made clear that these aren't just fringe left beliefs—there is mass support for left politics." Taube became deeply involved in Ocasio-Cortez's campaign, and then in Julia Salazar's successful campaign for New York State Senate, and after that, Tiffany Cabán's near-victory for district attorney of Queens. All three candidates were DSA members and endorsed by DSA.

Most DSA members who joined on the heels of the first Sanders campaign went through a similar politicization process. Tim Higginbotham of Anchorage, Alaska, who is twenty-seven, says, "I had never even attempted to become involved in politics and I generally ran from political conver-sations until Bernie's 2016 campaign. I remember watching a small Vermont town hall of his on YouTube the day he announced his candidacy and being blown away by his platform and persuasiveness." Higginbotham "had heard of DSA through social media, so I decided to pay my dues and start a DSA presence in Alaska because I knew that I wasn't going to be able to put out the socialist fire that Bernie sparked in my heart."

"I come from a family of hard workers," says twenty-four-year-old Bryan LaVergne of Houston, Texas the grandson of southern Louisiana sharecroppers. "My grandfather never voted a day in his life and never made it past the sixth grade. I grew up being told that determination and a hard sweat will get you to the right place." He worked as a technician in medical research for a few years, and saw "that the advancements of medical technology were often going to private companies to make a profit by turning the passion of researchers into treatments exclusive to those who can afford it." He continues,

When Bernie Sanders ran for president in the 2016 election, he taught me that I could no longer rely solely on the lessons of working hard in the system, but that instead we must all struggle together in changing the institutions that profit off of our exploitation.

With Hillary Clinton's loss to Donald Trump, I knew I could no longer wait to act. I attended my first DSA meeting in 2016 and witnessed democracy in action: members deliberated together before me, collectively deciding on political action. I felt the spark and have been an active member of DSA ever since, organizing alongside my chapter and the people of Houston. Every day I am fighting to build a world where no one will have to struggle like my grandparents did in Louisiana, where no one will go without health care because they can't afford it, where everyone is able to live a fully expressive and dignified life as a human in an ecologically sustainable world.

By mid-2017, DSA was a different entity than the one that existed two years prior. This new formation was ideologically diverse, but united in its disdain for business-as-usual

Democratic Party politics—which it identified as inadequate to combating the mounting threat of the Right under a Trump presidency—and its goal of making socialism mainstream.

Local chapters immediately undertook an enormous amount of non-electoral work. Much of it consisted of setting up shop, through activities like building chapter infrastructure, writing bylaws and forming committees, staging internal debates and holding elections, and organizing political education for members. But a great deal of it also consisted of local and national organizing projects, designed to raise DSA's profile while also cohering working-class political constituencies and building pressure for socialist demands, from Medicare for All to fair union contracts for workers to ending evictions.

Over the next two years, chapters undertook their own organizing work, guided by assessments of local conditions and priorities that chapter members democratically decided on. In San Francisco, DSA members who worked at Anchor Brewing, the biggest factory in the city, organized a union alongside their coworkers, with the support of their chapter. In Providence, Rhode Island, DSA members organized a campaign to take back the city's electrical power from the multinational utilities company National Grid Ventures by municipalizing it, and won reductions for low-income ratepayers in the process. After Austin DSA's campaign for paid sick days pressured the city council to pass the first paid sick leave policy in the South, other Texas chapters followed suit. Nationally, the organization prioritized Medicare for All, building infrastructure to share resources with chapters so they could mount local campaigns for single-payer health care, often in connection with local health care–related campaigns like Austin's.

Madeline Detelich of Austin, aged twenty-eight, describes how her politics matured and her commitment to socialism deepened in the process of working on Austin's paid sick leave campaign,

> I was invited by someone who was invited by his union steward to my first DSA meeting, which was the December 2016 general body meeting. It was packed. I didn't understand the significance of the 2016 Sanders campaign, but ended up voting for him simply because I knew climate change would never be addressed without bold solutions. However, in the confusion and despair of Trump's victory, I immediately knew that I was in the right place.
>
> I attended a few more meetings in 2017, but I seriously committed in January 2018 when my chapter ran a paid sick days campaign. I think it was a combination of getting my first taste of canvassing, and victory, as well as seeing the fierce opposition to something that I could clearly see the importance of. I had gone many years at that point without paid sick leave, so I was familiar with the mental math one does to see if they can afford to miss a day, even when you know that everyone would benefit from containing the contagion.
>
> When I was attending the occasional meeting and even for a while after I officially joined, I didn't think of myself as a socialist. I had been consuming anti-capitalist memes and Reddit posts, but I didn't have a grasp on an alternative. Organizing with DSA has improved my understanding of politics, and the more I learn, the more committed to the movement I become.

As the group's membership numbers continued to grow, its imprint on American politics grew, too—demonstrating the outsize impact a proportionally small group of committed organizers can have in a bleak political landscape, where most citizens don't see politics as part of their daily lives and most politicians are completely divorced from an organic and active working-class base. Mainstream media took major notice. In 2017, the *New York Times* asked, "Why Are So Many Young Voters Falling for Old Socialists?" CNN: "Democratic Socialists Are Taking Themselves Seriously. Should Democrats?" *Huffington Post*: "Is Democratic Socialists of America the Future of the Left?"

Throughout the early years of DSA's growth, Bernie Sanders also refused to recede from the public eye, cementing his status as one of the most recognizable people in the United States and, according to polls, the nation's most well-liked politician. He used his growing recognition to continue talking about class, corporate power, and democratic social-ism. There's no way to know which contributed more to DSA's growth during this period: the group's own public-facing activism and organizing work, or the catalytic effect of Bernie's high-profile advocacy for a new American class politics. Surely it was a combination of both—Sanders opened people's eyes to the class war already underway, and DSA gave people a way to meaningfully fight back.

DSA received another huge influx of members in July 2018, precipitated by the primary election victory of Ocasio-Cortez. Oren Schweitzer of New York City, who is now eighteen, joined as part of this wave. "I had been a Bernie supporter in 2016 when I was a high school freshman and had been involved with social justice work in school. After Alexandria Ocasio-Cortez won her primary, I began to read more about Ocasio-Cortez, DSA, and democratic socialism." Schweitzer went on to participate in campaigns for DSA members Julia Salazar and Tiffany Cabán, and is currently organizing a Young Democratic Socialists of America chapter at his college.

Ocasio-Cortez's campaign video, written by her and directed by DSA members, dripped with class-struggle rhetoric:

> Women like me aren't supposed to run for office. I wasn't born to a wealthy or powerful family . . . My name is Alexandria Ocasio-Cortez. I'm an educator, an organizer, a working-class New Yorker . . . After 20 years of the same representation, we have to ask: Who has New York been changing for? Every day gets harder for working families like mine to get by. The rent gets higher, health care covers less, and our income stays the same. It's clear that these changes haven't been for us.

Ocasio-Cortez became an overnight media sensation—not least because the charismatic young socialist struck terror into the heart of the political Right. Ocasio-Cortez's and DSA's stars rose together; again, mainstream media noticed. After Ocasio-Cortez's victory, the *New York Times* had more questions: "Are You a Democratic Socialist?" NPR gave you "What You Need to Know about the Democratic Socialists of America." *USA Today* summed it up boldly: "Capitalism Only Works for the Rich. We Deserve to Share the Wealth: Democratic Socialists."

While Ocasio-Cortez retains some ties to DSA, she's completely autonomous from the organization in practice. However, in a testament to her own political instincts, that lack of formal accountability to the socialist movement didn't stop her from immediately using her newfound celebrity to agitate for an ambitious short-term agenda that mirrored DSA's, and to speak openly about the class divide in America and its implications for politics and daily life. For example, when asked how we would pay for Medicare for All, Ocasio-Cortez effortlessly responded live on CNN:

> Why is it that our pockets are only empty when it comes to education and health care for our kids? Why are our pockets only empty when we talk about 100 percent renewable energy that is going to save this planet and allow our children to thrive? We only have empty pockets when it comes to the morally right things to do, but when it comes to tax cuts for billionaires and when it comes to unlimited war, we seem to be able to invent that money very easily.

The press made much out of Ocasio-Cortez's DSA connection. A lot of the coverage was surprisingly positive, evidence of a (inevitably short-lived) window of tolerance for socialist ideas in the mainstream media, if for no other reason than that such ideas were novel and seemed to emerge out of nowhere for many journalists. However, centrist news outlets also routinely downplayed the organization's radical politics, assuring readers and viewers that democratic socialism was synonymous with a tepid variant of New Deal–style social democracy and posed no existential threat to capitalism.

DSA members took the opportunity to correct this misunderstanding and explain our objection to capitalism, viewing the confusion from the center and the attacks from the Right as an opportunity to talk about the inherent flaws of a system that requires some people to sell their labor on the open market while others reap the profits of that labor.

By the time the midterms were over, Ocasio-Cortez had been joined by DSA member Rashida Tlaib of Michigan in Congress, and the number of DSA members had surged to 55,000.

Despite the truly stunning amount of media coverage, the astonishing rate at which public consciousness rose around policies like Medicare for All, and even a new openness toward embracing the word "socialism," DSA is not in a position to take over the state or civil society any time soon. The organization nevertheless does have opportunities that didn't exist before. Democratic socialism is gaining recognition and legitimacy, people are becoming politicized and radicalized in unprecedented numbers, and we have a shot at funneling that new energy into real fighting institutions, instead of simply watching it diffuse as it did after the initial upsurge of Occupy Wall Street.

Since the organization's rebirth, DSA has been minting socialist cadre—militant, politically developed, and fully dedicated organizers—in numbers not seen in half a century or more in the United States. Tens of thousands of people who had been left-leaning liberals, unaffiliated socialists, or apolitical began showing up in DSA spaces, where leaders have engaged them in external-facing campaigns that teach them vital organizing skills, as well as political education programs that teach them class analysis in the Marxist tradition.

Most members of DSA are paper members, who at most occasionally turn up for protests or volunteer infrequently on individual campaigns that pique their interest. But hundreds of members, perhaps even thousands, have become cadre, devoting what waking hours they can to the cause of building DSA and spreading socialism, even sometimes changing jobs to better accommodate this task—going into strategic unionized sectors to become rank-and-file activists, for example.

Since the two major US political parties are not really parties in any traditional sense (no membership criteria, no binding democratic decision-making, no political education, no discipline of candidates, no accountability to a platform), socialist cadre are some of the only people in the United States—excluding full-time, professional organizers and campaign staffers—who are trained as dedicated political actors. Very few people who aren't paid to do so spend all their time thinking about how to build their forces, persuade masses of people to adopt their perspective, and organize campaigns to win their politics. In this vacuum, the small number of socialist cadre have outsized influence in the political sphere.

By late 2019, the organization's membership was over ten times the size it was before Sanders first announced his presidential campaign. While much of DSA's organizing activity remains non-electoral, there are many socialists in the organization who take contesting for state power seriously. And their dominant orientation toward electoral politics is class-struggle elections.

3

Socialists in Action

While socialists are feeling optimistic about our recent surge, we're also cautious. We're still a small minority with a limited capacity. Our electoral victories have been inspiring, but there aren't that many of them. And the victories that *have* been clinched by Democratic Socialists of America (DSA) members have come in ones and twos: two members of the House of Representatives (Rashida Tlaib and Alexandria Ocasio-Cortez); a state legislator here (Lee Carter in Virginia and Julia Salazar in New York, among others) and a judge (Franklin Bynum in Houston) or city council member there (Dean Preston in San Francisco; Candi CdeBaca in Denver; Seema Singh Perez in Knoxville, Tennessee; Joel Sipress in Duluth, Minnesota; Denise Joy in Billings, Montana; Sean Parker in Nashville; Tristan Rader in Lakewood, Ohio, and others).

Even those of us who are serious about winning are trying to be realistic about our chances. But the successes we've achieved in some recent elections indicate that now is not the time to hold back. Instead, it is precisely the right time to take our chances—challenging elites, building coalitions, raising expectations, popularizing socialist ideas, and empowering ordinary working-class people in the process, whether we win or lose.

In this chapter, we take up some case studies from socialist electoral campaigns in three metropolitan areas. In Chicago, a willingness to endorse a large slate of candidates for city council ended up paying off, with half a dozen of them winning. In California's East Bay (covering Oakland, Berkeley, and several other cities east of San Francisco), the Jovanka Beckles campaign for State Assembly showed how a campaign can fall short electorally but still build power on the ground. And in New York City, several successful campaigns for national and state office showed how socialists can play key roles as part of a broader working-class coalition to win enormous progressive victories.

We chose these cities because Micah lives in Chicago and Meagan lives in the East Bay—meaning we got to witness and participate in these campaigns—while New York City has been the single most active hub of socialist electoral activity in the past few years. But socialists are running for office all over the country, from Maryland to Texas to Washington, in places urban and suburban and rural, and adjusting their strategies to the political climate accordingly. We think that's exactly what they should be doing, and we hope the stories here will embolden others to follow their example.

Despite being an eternal disappointment to the majority of people, the capitalist-allied political establishment is able to remain in power in part by maintaining the illusion that politics is for experts, people with Rolodexes full of professional contacts, people who went to elite schools. Since the myth of meritocracy maintains that people get ahead professionally because they're smarter or better than others, the people who are in charge (both as candidates and behind the scenes) are presumed deserving of their pedestal—and the proof of their deservingness is precisely that they're in charge. It's a dizzying tautology.

The truth is that the people who engage in politics professionally are not inherently smarter than everybody else. (In fact, through engaging with the process up close, we've learned that many of them are actually dumber.) And when they turn their backs on principles of equality and justice, they demonstrate that they don't deserve to be in the drivers' seat. They do have some specialized knowledge, but ordinary people can develop that knowledge themselves through collective trial and error. If we don't muster the courage to challenge the establishment, they'll run the show forever. If we want politics to change, it's time to roll up our sleeves.

Chicago

The 2019 socialist victories in Chicago are the clearest indication that a big, bold electoral strategy can actually win. Six members of the Democratic Socialists of America were elected to the Chicago city council in April 2019: Carlos Ramirez-Rosa, Rossana Rodriguez, Byron Sigcho-Lopez, Jeanette Taylor, Andre Vasquez, and Daniel La Spata. This means that 12 percent of the fifty-member council are DSA members.

When Chicago DSA (CDSA) began thinking about how it would approach the 2019 election cycle, many members counseled a conservative approach. Only one DSA member, Carlos Ramirez-Rosa, was running for reelection. All other socialists running for city council would have to topple incumbents, several of whom had held office for decades or were part of long-standing local political dynasties. Many in the chapter argued to endorse one or two campaigns and throw everything behind winning them.

Yet CDSA did not do this. The chapter didn't endorse every candidate who came calling (including one candidate and DSA member, Daniel La Spata, who ultimately ended up winning). But the group decided to cast a wide net, endorsing five candidates for city council: Sigcho-Lopez, Taylor, Ramirez-Rosa, Rodriguez, and Ugo Okere.

The eventual results were shocking: Ramirez-Rosa won his election outright, by nearly twenty percentage points; Sigcho-Lopez, Taylor, and Rodriguez advanced to a second round of runoff elections and won. Okere lost in the first round, but another DSA member running in that same ward, Andre Vasquez, advanced to the runoff; CDSA quickly endorsed him (as did Okere), and Vasquez won in the second round.

CDSA opted for audacity rather than timidity. That audacity paid off. "It turns out that as we endorsed more candidates, our capacity grew rather than shrank," Steve Weishampel, at the time the CDSA's electoral working group co-chair, wrote after the elections.

The successful campaigns shared a few key characteristics. The candidates had a core message in common: fight the wealthy and their political lackeys pushing gentrification and austerity in Chicago. The six races spanned much of Chicago and a wide range of neighborhood-specific issues, but all the candidates signed onto a broad, left platform: housing for all, sanctuary for all, education for all, and taxing the rich. These demands reflected political issues and movement demands in Chicago, but are also burning issues throughout the country.

And they were united in a political approach that wasn't afraid to name the class enemy in the city, especially the real estate developers that are rapidly gentrifying working-class neighborhoods and forcing working people out of Chicago.

Ramirez-Rosa, for example, made his race a referendum on affordable housing and gentrification, a pressing issue in his ward, where rents are rapidly rising. He painted real estate developers as the enemy of the ward's working class. The real estate developers responded by painting *him* as the enemy. The ward's largest landlord, Mark Fishman, spent at least $100,000 on Ramirez-Rosa's opponent in an effort to unseat him; other developers, big landlords, and property managers spent an additional $100,000. Voters were flooded with attack mailers—DSA canvassers often saw them stacked high on porches and in apartment building vestibules—leveling wild accusations that Ramirez-Rosa was a deadbeat city council member and that he didn't actually care about affordable housing in the ward. They didn't work.

"In corporate politics the narrative is you can screw over the voters, you can screw the working class, and as long as you have the money to get on TV and slam your opponents in the mail boxes, you can win," Ramirez-Rosa said after the election. "We turned that logic upside down—not just in my ward, but in wards across Chicago, where we saw corporate Democrats spending big and losing. At the end of the day, if you reach the voters door to door with a compelling message and a political vision that speaks to their needs, they're going to go with you every time."

Ramirez-Rosa's campaign didn't shy away from attacking the ward's most powerful capitalist. That class-struggle approach paid off: he won reelection by nearly 20 percent over his real estate–friendly opponent.

Ramirez-Rosa's win and the other five victories didn't come in a vacuum. All six of the candidates are DSA members, but they are also aligned with unions, community groups, political organizations, and other groups. Those groups both paved the way for these victories and played key roles during the campaign. And DSA showed them that socialists are key allies in these fights.

All of the candidates were endorsed by United Working Families (UWF), the political organization formed by the Chicago Teachers Union (CTU) and SEIU Healthcare Illinois-Indiana along with a number of community groups, which other unions and community organizations have joined in recent years. It also devoted significant resources to many of the campaigns. Most unions and progressive groups shy away from the "socialist" label. UWF didn't.

In addition to UWF's support, Rodriguez had the backing of a neighborhood group, 33rd Ward Working Families, that had run teacher and socialist Tim Meegan for the office in 2015. Since then, the group has organized around affordable housing and immigrants' rights in a working-class immigrant neighborhood, Albany Park—so effectively that the losing incumbent, Deb Mell, complained that 33rd Ward Working Families "never stopped running over the last four years." Mell, a hapless hack whose father gave her the city council seat in the middle of his term in 2013 after holding it himself for nearly four decades, apparently thought candidates who organize in their communities are cheating. After her victory the *Chicago Sun-Times* christened Rodriguez a "dynasty slayer."

UWF and the rest of Chicago wouldn't be willing to elect leftist candidates if the city hadn't been such a hotbed of working-class militancy in recent years. The CTU's 2012 strike brought a sea change to city politics, popularizing opposition to austerity and making the union the city's most important force in that fight. The CTU's willingness to strike—in public schools, as it did again for a single day in an illegal strike in 2016 and in a long, open-ended strike in 2019, and in charters, where it organized aggressively and struck repeatedly after 2012—has reshaped the city's politics (and helped make all kinds of workers, from graduate teaching assistants to the Chicago Symphony Orchestra, more willing to withhold their labor from the boss).

That militancy is also seen in CTU-adjacent community groups like the Kenwood Oakland Community Organization (KOCO), of which Jeanette Taylor has been an active member for many years. KOCO is a mostly black organization based in black neighborhoods on the city's South Side that has long fought education austerity. Their organizing helped inspire the group of reformers within the CTU that took over the union's leadership in 2010 and pushed it in a more radical direction, committed to fighting for the city's entire working class (especially in black and Latino neighborhoods) rather than just teachers themselves. KOCO led a month-long hunger strike in 2015 demanding the reopening of a neighborhood high school. Taylor was one of the hunger strikers. "The movement made and pushed me," Taylor said before she was elected. "I don't like doing all this, running for office and talking in public. That's something I was molded into doing."

In other words, CDSA should be credited for being audacious enough to run five socialists for city council, and for playing key roles—in several cases, the central role—in the victorious campaigns. But DSA didn't win these victories on its own. The group was part of a broad working-class movement that tied electoral campaigns to grassroots labor and community organizing and militancy. Without that wider ferment in the city, it's doubtful the six socialists would have won their seats.

The lesson from Chicago, then, is not just that you can run socialist candidates who take on the ruling class and actually win, and not just that you can run *many* socialist candidates and win. It's also that socialists must join (or start) fights at their workplaces and in their communities that can create the broader political conditions for electoral victories. Those fights, built painstakingly over years and even decades in the city, created the conditions in which six socialists could win city council seats—and shortly after the election, CDSA's then co-chairs Leonard Pierce and Lucie Macias could declare in the *Chicago Tribune*, "Chicago's politicians and the ultra-wealthy, from the mayor's office to corporate boardrooms, need to understand that business isn't going to continue as usual in this city."

It's impossible to know what will come of these wins. At the time of this writing, the six socialists have held office for less than a year. The city's capitalist class, like capitalists everywhere, is very powerful. And because CDSA doesn't have many institutional mechanisms to force its candidates to remain faithful to a socialist program, it's possible that the rich could pick off a few of the socialist victors. A key task going forward will be figuring out how to not just win city council campaigns like these, but keep victorious city council members from succumbing to capitalist or mainstream Democratic Party pressure.

But in the immediate aftermath of the victory, things look promising. The city council socialists have hit the streets: Rodriguez has used her megaphone to support tenants organizing against abusive landlords in the neighborhood and provided space for numerous working-class organizing efforts in her ward. Several of the new council members have used their office to organize against Donald Trump's threatened ICE raids in Chicago. The newly elected leaders even joined in blocking traffic outside City Hall to protest massive giveaways to real estate developers shortly after the elections. A "Socialist Caucus" on the fifty-member city council is in its infancy, one that will hopefully be more politically principled and consistent than the "Progressive Caucus," whose members can't be relied on to speak as a bloc on much of anything. And all six endorsed Bernie Sanders for president.

And all of the six could be seen on the picket lines during the CTU's 2019 strike. They coauthored a *Chicago Sun-Times* op-ed siding with the teachers over the mayor and demanding that Chicago's schools be adequately funded—no small development in a city where the city council's complete fealty to the mayor could previously be taken for granted. Chicago's elected officials are using their office to stoke more grassroots organizing, more bottom-up opposition to austerity, more class struggle.

The political conditions in Chicago are unique, of course. So are every city's. But there's no reason other cities can't wage local electoral campaigns that name our enemy, the capitalist class, and that work and grow alongside militant working-class organizing.

East Bay

In California's East Bay in 2018, the local DSA chapter aimed high for their first electoral campaign and tried to put a democratic socialist in a state-level office. They lost, but only narrowly, and in the end they had a lot to show for it. Their story shows that socialists shouldn't be afraid to take risks when choosing to mount a class-struggle campaign, even if victory isn't certain.

Winning office is important, of course. Without concrete victories, we can't hope to sustain ourselves in electoral work, and we can't hope to jolt millions of people out of their acquiescence to a way of politics that they know isn't working for them, but which they believe can't be transcended.

Electoral victories themselves also aren't enough. If socialists run winning campaigns but fail to use them to fortify class movements, then having the right people in office means very little. That's only half the battle. The other half has to focus on shifting the balance of class power. As left electoral efforts have historically shown, personal allegiances are a poor match for impersonal social forces. The only way to ensure a candidate with strong personal fidelity to the working-class movement can resist capitalism's conservatizing pressures is to organize outside the state, in ways that create the conditions to allow left-elected leaders to succeed and that ensure those leaders can be held accountable to the movements they emerged from and belong to.

With that bigger picture in mind, socialists should not be afraid to lose electoral contests, so long as the campaign has been successful in polarizing, politicizing, and picking fights on a large scale.

The 2018 campaign of Jovanka Beckles for California State Assembly District 15 (spanning from Richmond through Berkeley and down to Oakland) offers a case study in how to wage class struggle on the campaign trail, and how social-ists can use those campaigns—even when they're not successful in winning office—to strengthen their own skillsets and relationships and apply them to workers' struggles on the ground.

Jovanka Beckles is a DSA member, a queer black Latina immigrant, a county social worker, and a member of Team-sters Local 856. For eight years, she sat on the city council of Richmond, a small working-class city north of Berkeley,

California. There, she was instrumental in battling Chevron, which has an oil refinery based in Richmond and is the city's largest employer, largest polluter, and most egregious tax avoider.

East Bay DSA endorsed and developed a close relationship with Beckles in the lead-up to the assembly election. Chapter members worked with her on her platform and her speeches, and staffed her campaign. In political collaboration with East Bay DSA, Beckles's campaign emphasized corporate domination, capitalist exploitation, and working-class power. Hers was hands down the most radical and inspiring platform in California in 2018.

Beckles's platform called for the kinds of policies all socialists should call for: universal rent control and mass public construction of social housing, universal single-payer health care, fully funded public education and a moratorium on charter school expansion, public childcare and tuition-free public universities, a shorter work week and stronger union protections, a $20 minimum wage, abolition of cash bail and private prisons, strong environmental regulations at the expense of corporate profits, and new taxes on the rich. But what was special about Beckles's campaign wasn't just her platform: it was the sincere promise at the heart of the campaign that she would represent and fight to strengthen the movement of working people against the capitalist class.

Beckles's opponent, Buffy Wicks, had never before been elected to office, but was a veteran of the Obama and Clinton campaigns, as well as the world of PACs and political and professional consulting. As a California staffer for Clinton's presidential campaign in 2016, she was nicknamed "Buffy the Bernie Slayer" for her role in helping Clinton defeat Sanders in the state's primary. In short order, the real estate, tech, and charter school industries lined up behind Wicks, investing millions of dollars into independent expenditure funds to elect Wicks and defeat Beckles.

East Bay DSA chose to treat the open capitalist support for Wicks as an opportunity for agitation. The chapter built a website, buffywicks.money, which named all the corporate donors to Wicks's campaign and exposed their ties to big industry, to the Democratic Party establishment, and even to the Republican Party and the Trump Administration. The website put the Wicks campaign on the defensive—and more importantly it pointed to an opponent bigger than just Wicks herself: capitalists.

Beckles campaigned as an open democratic socialist critical of capitalism, exposing hundreds of thousands of people to a socialist worldview. In an interview with *Jacobin* she said,

Capitalism isn't working for us. It's only working for the few, and we need a new economy that works for the many. Democratic socialism is about understanding that we do have the resources to be able to provide everything that we need. Not only do we have those resources, we *create* them as working people.

We can have free and good quality housing, health care, childcare, education, and more, but our current for-profit system won't give it to us. Capitalism gives us homeless people sleeping in cities with vacant housing units. It gives us people dying because their insurance company refused to pay for a simple procedure. That's what we get from a system that puts profit over people.

Socialism means putting people over profit, so we can have the society we're all dreaming of. And it's possible. It's not far-fetched.

Beckles's campaign was East Bay DSA's first electoral rodeo. Throughout the process, chapter members built skills from canvass captaining to political writing and design. The chapter's own internal operations were greatly strengthened through the process of conducting the campaign for Beckles. And the campaign helped put the chapter on the map, as DSA members were front and center in the campaign and Beckles wasn't shy about identifying herself as one.

Beckles received over ninety thousand votes. That's more than Alexandria Ocasio-Cortez and Rashida Tlaib combined. However, Wicks outspent Beckles six to one, and Beckles narrowly lost.

The loss stung for East Bay DSA, of course. But because the socialists in that chapter didn't see elections as a simple means to an end of putting a socialist in office, the class-struggle orientation that propelled the campaign provided a kind of continuity: if enemy number one wasn't Buffy Wicks but the capitalist class, then that class was still dominant no matter who won. Either way, the fight continued.

Within a month, East Bay DSA had begun to channel the energy from the Beckles campaign into the Oakland teachers' contract fight against the Oakland Unified School District, a local iteration of the national teachers' strike wave. Not coincidentally, the opponents in the new fight were the same as the previous one. The Oakland school board was staffed by pro-privatization members whose political careers are funded by the same forces who backed Wicks. Some of their donors were the *same individuals* profiled on buffywicks.money.

The chapter had built a tightly organized operation during the campaign. Usually after an electoral campaign ends, people scatter to the winds. But East Bay DSA took all of that energy and experience—and the institutional competency and cohesion that, if left idle, tends to wane in the months after elections—and used it to organize for the next battle.

As a strike loomed, East Bay DSA assembled a group for Oakland public school teachers who were also DSA members to strategize about how they would share the socialist perspective with their coworkers during the strike. The chapter started organizing house parties for parents and community members, and partnering with the union in organizing pre-strike canvasses. The canvasses sent socialists and teachers side by side into Oakland's working-class neighborhoods, bringing signs designed by an East Bay DSA member to doors that people could put up. Eventually, the signs blanketed the city.

East Bay DSA organized a panel that brought leaders from Los Angeles, which had just won their own massive and successful teachers' strike, to Oakland to share their perspective. When high school students staged a pre-strike walkout in support of their teachers, East Bay DSA was there to provide security. When teachers held a pre-strike rally to drum up community support, the chapter was there, too—and when Buffy Wicks showed up, members of East Bay DSA filmed themselves asking her where she got the nerve, given her charter school connections. Wicks left the scene without speaking to the crowd, and the chapter posted the video online.

The chapter also created an independent online publication called *East Bay Majority* devoted to advancing a socialist viewpoint on the strike. This publication contributed heavily to the public pressure campaign on the school district, and introduced teachers and parents to socialists' class-based perspective. East Bay DSA launched a massive fundraiser called Bread for Ed, collecting nearly $200,000 to feed children during the strike at solidarity schools, so that low-income students wouldn't have to cross the picket line in order to get lunch. Bread for Ed also fed teachers during the mid-day strike rallies.

When the strike came, the chapter borrowed an old labor organizing strategy and coordinated with the union to organize "flying squadrons" of its members to strengthen picket lines every morning of the strike at 6:30 a.m. The union would give the chapter information about what lines seemed weak, and cars full of socialists would arrive to bulk them up. They walked the picket lines every day of the strike, joining in chants, talking politics, and providing supplies where needed. And, of course, Jovanka Beckles was there herself in the streets supporting striking teachers.

In his role as both a veteran Oakland teacher of twenty-two years and a DSA member, union member Tim Marshall was able to closely observe the relationship between the two groups. In an interview in the heat of the strike, Marshall said,

The support of younger socialists has been crucial. It's not like how it used to be, with radicals isolated in their unions, the residual effects of the Cold War and red-baiting forcing them to disguise their politics. DSA is much more out front.

The role that East Bay DSA has played has been really welcome in the union. There are DSA members who are teachers on the organizing committee, and there were DSA members out on picket lines all over town this morning. In the lead-up to the strike DSA has cosponsored events with the union and taken on a huge logistical burden to make them happen. Bread for Ed, a massive fundraiser to feed kids during the strike, would not have happened without DSA. Much of the solidarity school organizing would not have happened without DSA.

The other day I had an exchange with our union president Keith Brown. I said, "Thank you for all you do," and he responded, "No thank you brother. You brought the squad." And by the squad he meant DSA.

None of East Bay DSA's solidarity work would have been possible without the infrastructure the chapter had built and the political lessons and skills its members had learned during the Beckles campaign. And crucially, the strike solidarity campaign was guided by the same political mission as that of the Beckles campaign. East Bay DSA members emphasized that this was just a new chapter in the ongoing fight against the same class.

In the end, the teachers forced district leaders to cede an 11 percent raise, won a small reduction in class sizes, and secured a moratorium on charter school expansion. It was far from a total victory, and East Bay DSA members and other observers tried to be honest about that. But concessions gained can't be our only measure of success, because most strikes end in some kind of compromise. Most importantly, Oakland's teachers' strike energized and transformed tens of thousands of teachers, students, and community members to fight for more. Educators felt their own power—and they recognized their class enemies. In the process, East Bay DSA grew closer to union militants (several of whom have since joined DSA) and learned major lessons and even more skills through class-struggle organizing on the ground.

Oakland teachers, parents, and students have continued to push back against the school board's plans for school closures and privatization; for example, they staged an action in October 2019 that elicited a violent police response, drawing national attention to the crisis. Additionally, when Oakland students walked out en masse during the climate strikes later in 2019, they and the teachers who helped them coordinate their actions drew from their organizing experiences and networks formed during the teachers' strike. The strike energized thousands of people new to activism, equipped them with confidence and skills, and emboldened them to keep fighting. And the struggle could develop new electoral expressions, too, as the Oakland Education Association and East Bay DSA coordinate with each other to identify left-wing candidates to run for school board.

While we can't assert direct causality, we can draw a line from the Jovanka Beckles campaign through the Oakland teachers' strike to the teacher, parent, and student resistance that continues in Oakland today. All are iterations of escalating working-class resistance in the East Bay, with organized socialists playing key support roles—and accumulating skills and confidence as the fight continues.

This demonstrates a central tenet of class-struggle electoral politics: the fight neither begins nor ends at the ballot box. Contests for state power are part of a continuous project to empower working people to self-organize. Candidates and the socialists who help run their campaigns must be devoted to inspiring and bolstering working-class movements outside the state, whether or not that candidate wins on election day.

The lesson: try in earnest to win, but take risks and don't be afraid to lose. After all, Bernie Sanders lost his 2016 bid for the presidency, but he still changed American politics in the process. As long as socialists have built up the momentum of working-class movements in the course of running an electoral campaign, that campaign was well worth the effort.

New York

New York has been the site of the most important electoral campaign win yet: Ocasio-Cortez's insurgent run for the House in 2018, which we introduced in the previous chapter. Her victory led to an explosion of membership in DSA nationally, the biggest jump in membership after the Sanders campaign and Donald Trump's victory. It also led to a sea change in American politics, putting critical issues like a Green New Deal on the public agenda. Less examined, however, is how Ocasio-Cortez's win was part of a massive shift in the politics of New York City and New York State.

Her victory, along with Julia Salazar's in the New York State Senate, were, in the grand scheme of their respective legislative bodies, small—Salazar was the lone socialist in a body of sixty-three; Ocasio-Cortez, one of two with Rashida Tlaib of Michigan out of 435. Yet Ocasio-Cortez's and Salazar's victories, combined with the continued organizing efforts and electoral victories of the socialist and broader working-class movement that put them in office, quickly effected a massive shift in New York politics that produced huge victories against two of the most powerful capitalists in the world today: real estate developers and Amazon.

Ocasio-Cortez's story is a true pull-yourself-up-by-your-bootstraps tale: a bartender who had grown up in and around the Bronx went up against a major power broker in the Democratic Party who assumed he would be next in line for his party's most important position in the House of

Representatives. Instead, Ocasio-Cortez knocked him off and headed to Capitol Hill. Pandemonium ensued. Ocasio-Cortez was the subject of nonstop press coverage, her utterances and tweets regularly calling the tune of the day's news cycle. She instantly became an icon of the rising US Left, and right-wing media became obsessed, hanging onto her every word.

Salazar's path to victory wasn't quite as straight. She campaigned as an unabashed democratic socialist, foregrounding her membership in the DSA and her opposition to capitalism, centering the need to fight the absurdly high rents and displacement in her rapidly gentrifying Brooklyn district and even suggesting she didn't believe that the Democratic Party could ever be realigned in a more progressive direction. Salazar was dogged by questions about inconsistencies in her biography, leading to an incredible depth of media scrutiny, unprecedented in a state senate race. The intense hostility Salazar faced was undoubtedly provoked by her uncompromising left-wing stances, including her stance in favor of the boycott, divestment, and sanctions (BDS) movement, which is seen as a major threat to the state of Israel and thus draws attacks against any politician who backs it, even at the city and state level. She was even involuntarily outed by a right-wing American media outlet, in a bizarre and cruel apparent attempt to discredit her as a candidate, as a victim of sexual assault in 2013 by an Israeli spokesperson for the prime minister.

And, yet, despite the vicious attacks, Salazar won. "This is a victory for workers," she told her supporters on election night.

New York now had only two socialists in elected office: one in the House of Representatives, one in the state senate. But the presence of two of them, as part of a broader progressive upsurge in the state, would soon have massive consequences. Salazar's election was part of a wave of state senate primary races that unseated the Independent Democratic Conference (IDC), a group of six state senators who were Democrats but voted with the Republican Party, often denying the Democrats in the state legislature a majority. The IDC senators' losses were proof that "the progressive fervor sweeping national politics had hobbled New York's once-mighty Democratic machine, at least on a local level," the *New York Times* wrote the day after the election.

Of course, simply defeating one group of Democrats and replacing them with another wasn't guaranteed to change politics in the state. That sea change came from Ocasio-Cortez and Salazar, and the clear message that DSA spread through its electoral work. As then NYC DSA co-chair Abdullah Younus put it, "We don't want real estate money in our political system." More broadly, New York voters were rejecting pro-corporate politics.

"Every elected official . . . was constantly looking over their shoulder for a left primary challenge, and was legislating from that perspective," NYC DSA member Aaron Taube said about the period after the two victories. This spelled bad news for one of the world's largest and most powerful companies, Amazon.

Sad Bezos

In September 2017, Amazon announced it was seeking a site for a new major headquarters. The "HQ2," along with its jobs and office space lease payments, would go to whichever city could eat enough shit to please Amazon's corporate overlords.

Soon after promising $2.5 billion in tax subsidies to lure the company to Chicago, neoliberal mayor extraordinaire

Rahm Emanuel sent a bizarre email to an Amazon executive bragging about the package by asking, "Whose [*sic*] your daddy?" A business group from Tucson, Arizona, sent a twenty-one-foot cactus to the Amazon Seattle headquarters. And in New York City, the night before the deadline for bidding, Mayor Bill de Blasio "lit every light he could, from the rooftops of One World Trade and the Empire State Building to all of the city's wifi hotspots, in Amazon's signature shade of orange," Nicky Woolf wrote in the *New Statesman*.

The price tags, too, were massive: Maryland offered $8 billion; Pittsburgh, nearly $10 billion. If company CEO Jeff Bezos had told these leaders to strip naked and tear each other limb from limb in an Amazon-branded mud pit, they probably would've done that, too.

In recent decades, when American capitalists have wanted something, chances are they've gotten it. So when the company announced that it would choose Long Island City, Queens, as its location, most observers assumed that was that.

The corporate giveaways New York had offered amounted to a staggering $3 billion. And the announcement of the plan immediately sent housing prices in Long Island City through the roof, with ripple effects throughout Queens and all of New York City anticipated. But the plan was backed by both Mayor de Blasio and New York Governor Andrew Cuomo. Who would expect anything else from establishment leaders? For them, as State Senator Ron Kim, who represents parts of Queens, explained to a reporter, "We're living under feudalism of the Lord of Amazon."

But in the midst of the Amazon HQ2 bidding process, Ocasio-Cortez won her primary challenge against Crowley. That victory changed the political terrain. For one thing, "you have this mobilized base of people who participate in left political fights in Queens now," said Taube, who coordinated DSA's portion of the field operation for Ocasio-Cortez.

DSA was far from the only group involved in Ocasio-Cortez's campaign: she was first recruited to run by the group Justice Democrats, and a broad coalition of left groups supported her campaign. But Taube believes that DSA provided more canvassers than any other group. After Ocasio-Cortez won, Queens DSA now had the mobilized base of left activists that Taube mentioned—which would soon be activated again for the Amazon fight.

Likewise, Salazar's election had drawn a line in the sand for New York politicians: were you on the side of working-class renters, or New York's wealthy real estate developers? Salazar's district was in Brooklyn, not Queens. But in refusing real estate developer money and turning her election into a referendum on affordable housing in the city, Salazar's campaign helped cohere a citywide narrative in opposition to those developers' attempts to push working-class people out of the city—a narrative that then pulled other statewide politicians to the pro-tenant, anti-gentrification side, for fear of losing their reelection bids. Given that the Amazon HQ2 would accelerate the already rapid displacement of working-class New Yorkers from Queens, those elected officials—some of whom had even publicly expressed support for Amazon coming to New York in the past—would now take up the fight against HQ2.

In November 2018, Ocasio-Cortez was, unsurprisingly, speaking out strongly against Amazon. But so was State Senator Michael Gianaris, the Senate's new deputy majority leader—a position he was given because Joe Crowley, Queens political power broker, had just been defeated by Ocasio-Cortez. "If Joe Crowley was still in power as the head of [the] Queens

County [Democratic machine], and people still thought the machine-backed electeds were invincible, I doubt that people would have come out against this deal," Taube said.

Soon everyone was speaking out against the company—even de Blasio, now offering stern warnings against the company's anti-union stances: "There's gonna be tremendous pressure on Amazon to allow unionization, and I will be one of the people bringing that pressure."

In February 2019, Senator Gianaris was nominated to the Public Authorities Control Board (PACB), a body that Amazon would have to get through in order to get into Queens. The nomination was approved by the majority leader of the state senate—again, a nomination that wouldn't have happened without the successful push to defeat the IDC as well as Ocasio-Cortez knocking out Crowley just a few months earlier. Before a PACB vote, however, Amazon dropped a bombshell: after announcing to the world that they would be going to Queens, they pulled out.

Andrew Cuomo soon called it the "greatest tragedy" of his entire political career. The grassroots groups that opposed the plan—including NYC DSA—shed no tears for him. The latter issued a statement on the day Amazon pulled out: "Today New York's working class showed that big business and billionaires can't buy our city. New York belongs to the many, not the few."

The path from Ocasio-Cortez's electoral victory to Amazon pulling out of Queens was a complicated one. It involved:

1) the election of democratic socialists to both the House of Representatives and the New York State Senate,
2) a consistently anti-corporate and anti-gentrification message that was at the center of those socialist campaigns,

3) New York socialists working alongside progressive community and labor unions (and opposing some others),
4) a broader wave of electoral wins in the state senate against the IDC, which DSA was not officially involved in but the electoral narrative was fundamentally shaped by DSA's message, and
5) those electoral wins and the broader progressive upsurge they were a part of translating into pressure on key city and state leaders to come out against Amazon and its scheme to receive billions in public subsidies.

The story, in other words, is far more complicated than a group of socialists acting alone to halt a corporate behemoth in its tracks. DSA worked within a much broader coalition in these elections and in the Amazon fight that included community groups like CAAAV Organizing Asian Communities and Desis Rising Up and Moving, and labor groups like the Retail, Wholesale and Department Store Union and the Working Families Party. Still, socialists played a key role in the victory.

"The coalition would have existed without DSA," said Taube. "But we would not have won the campaign when we won it, if Mike Gianaris hadn't gotten himself on the PACB and said he was going to veto the subsidies and the funding [for Amazon]. He would not have done that if it weren't for this left electoral operation that existed in and around his district. He was afraid of a DSA-led field operation."

In the end, Amazon decided to move to New York City anyway. Only the company did so without receiving $3 billion in public subsidies, money that would otherwise go to public programs and projects. And it opted to move to an already gentrified part of Manhattan, Hudson Yards, rather than Queens, limiting the likelihood of working-class displacement.

The coalition that mobilized against HQ2 has said from the beginning that Amazon did not need public assistance to move any city. The company simply wanted to see who would place the highest bid, and how much public money it could soak up. As Ocasio-Cortez surmised on Twitter after the announcement of Amazon's move to Manhattan, "We were proven right."

A New Lease on Rent Laws

Defeating Amazon was astounding enough. But then came another battle in which New York's capitalists would suffer defeat: the historic passage of the Housing Stability and Tenant Protection Act of 2019, which extended and strengthened laws on rent control. The law, passed by the state legislature in June 2019, was a huge boon to the 2.4 million New Yorkers who live in rent-stabilized apartments, removing numerous loopholes that allowed landlords to raise rents even on those units protected by rent control laws, and protecting tenants from harassment and displacement.

Again, NYC DSA was far from the only or even the most important player in the passage of the new rent laws. New York's real estate developers have played a cartoonishly evil role in the city for years, and a vibrant tenants' movement has long organized to stop them. The victory was possible because of the larger sea of working-class organizers that New York socialists were swimming in—and because the other organizations in that sea weren't scared off by working with socialists.

Closing the pro-landlord loopholes in New York City required the approval of the state legislature in Albany, but the IDC Democrats there had made such legislative action impossible. "Between 2000 and 2016, the [real estate] industry contributed $83 million to elected officials in Albany. Cuomo himself received millions in campaign donations. The sense that Albany was owned by the real estate lobby had become so entrenched in voters' psyches that it seemed it would never change," wrote Michael Greenberg.

The anti-IDC efforts broke the spell. New York's tenant organizations seized the moment. Just before existing tenant protections were set to expire on June 14, 2019, tenant groups called for a mass civil disobedience in the state capitol in Albany on June 4. "They filled the capitol's grand central staircase, scattering fake $100 bills imprinted with the faces of the governor and various landlords and developers," Greenberg wrote; sixty-one people were arrested. Shortly after, Senate Majority Leader Andrea Stewart-Cousins pledged to back the bill. Despite Cuomo's objections, the bill passed.

"We were able to join a long-standing tenant movement with a new left electoral movement," Cea Weaver, a director of organizing and campaign manager at Upstate/Downstate Housing Alliance, said. "For a long time, politicians could be on the side of landlords and that's just the way it was. It's not that way anymore."

This was the same dynamic that had produced the electoral will to prevent Amazon from receiving massive amounts of public subsidies in exchange for coming to New York. Ocasio-Cortez and especially Salazar, and the socialist group they were members of, made the rejection of real estate developer money and opposition to gentrification a crystal-clear talking point in New York politics. DSA's participation in these electoral struggles gave it a chance to cement this principle in the political discourse in New York, even among politicians who didn't necessarily believe in it themselves. The successful organizing in elections, along with a broad working-class coalition, translated to successful campaigns in the streets.

4

The Dirty Break

As should be clear from the examples in the last chapter, a new socialist movement is cohering in the US, thanks in large part to the popular class politics of Bernie Sanders. But as that movement grows and progresses, it's bound to run into dangerous obstacles and thorny contradictions. The new US socialist movement is without a single "line" or monolithic political position. That's a strength of the movement, since none of us has all the answers. Still, many people in the movement, ourselves included, feel strongly about certain approaches to strategy. One approach we feel strongly about is what we call "the democratic road to socialism," or the idea that we need to make good use of the democratic structures and processes available to us (and to improve and expand them) in order to advance our cause.

A country like the United States has both a well-developed capitalist state, beholden to the capitalist class and armed to the teeth, and mechanisms for democratic participation in that state that allow people to exercise some measure of control over their representatives. Even though their choices are limited, their representatives are bought off by the rich, and the capitalist class holds the entire system hostage with the threat of devastating economic retaliation if things don't go their way, the system does have some basic democratic elements that its citizens largely affirm and occasionally participate in.

This is a tricky situation to navigate. If the democratic capitalist state were less developed, it might be possible to convince people to simply storm the gates, tear up the old rules, and start fresh in a socialist society. This is what socialists tried to do in Russia in 1917: the state was weak and after centuries of autocratic rule it didn't have much legitimacy in the eyes of most Russians, so revolutionaries could get popular support for scrapping it and starting over.

The United States is hardly an exemplary democracy, and socialists must push to further democratize elements of the state. But even if people are unhappy about much of our corrupt political system today, it does hold a strong degree of legitimacy in most citizens' minds. Despite Republicans' continued efforts to restrict the franchise, most people can vote, and they see the results of elections as basically lawful and valid. People often (rightfully) feel dejected and cynical about US electoral politics, but they don't consider the system so illegitimate that they're willing to risk their lives to destroy it anytime soon.

Mass numbers of people are going to treat elections as the main arena for their political frustrations and aspirations, at least for the time being. These are objective conditions over which we have no control. The question we must face is whether we join them in the democratic sphere, giving socialist and class-struggle character to fights playing out in the electoral arena, or sit those fights out and miss the opportunity to engage with people by getting in the ring ourselves.

The democratic road strategy does not assume that we'll simply stack up reforms until we look up one day and have socialism. Social change is more complicated than that, happening as it does in fits and starts, often with brief periods of great advance and long dry spells in between. Capitalists won't let us slowly but surely inch our way toward a new society; at some point, probably around the time our advances start decisively challenging their control over industry and their profits, they're going to try to tear us down by any means necessary.

But reforms do have a major role in building socialism, and not just for the purpose of spreading our message. By engaging in mass democratic politics, and electing politicians faithful to our movement who can spearhead the fight for real reform (including democratizing the current state), we can tip the balance of power in favor of the working class.

That balance is decidedly not tipped in our favor today. The power of the capitalist class is now so great that it can punish cities, states, and countries whose working-class movements have successfully won gains for workers against bosses. The punishment doesn't even have to be intentional: by simply following their mandate to maximize profits, employers are naturally inclined to close shops whose labor costs make them uncompetitive and move to regions where workers are less powerful, demoralizing movements and wreaking economic havoc on the people who fight back the hardest. This is the story of manufacturing in the United States, especially over recent decades—companies have constantly moved operations, first within the country, from high-wage markets to relatively low-wage ones, then across the border or overseas, to countries with even lower wages like Mexico or China. Bosses don't have to be evil to do this; the market compels them to. They may not want to tear down a community's economic foundation, but if they don't, their competitors will undercut them.

To stop this race-to-the-bottom cycle undercutting workers' power and lay the groundwork for revolutionary change, we must erode the power of the capitalist class. We can accomplish that by, for example, imposing capital controls—measures that stop the free movement of capital in response to changing social and economic conditions. But to pass economic reforms as significant as these, we can't just agitate in the streets, as important as that is. We have to be in power.

Luckily for us, while contesting for that power comes with plenty of dilemmas we must be careful to avoid, it's also a fantastic opportunity. Without capital on our side, the project of contesting for state power becomes by necessity a democratic one. We achieve success in the electoral sphere when we've won over masses of people to our political agenda. Elections can be used to build mass working-class movements, and the project of wielding state power can be used to clear the path for those movements as they confront their class enemies.

Chris Maisano describes the democratic road as a strategy that pursues "election of a left government (likely over multiple contested elections) mandated to carry out a fundamental transformation of the political economy, coordinated with a movement from below to build new institutions and organizations of popular power in society."

Eric Blanc offers a similar formulation. Eventually, after the Left has won significant gains at the ballot box and in civil society, the capitalist class will take the gloves off against socialists and do whatever it takes to destroy our movement. We'll need to fight back. The democratic road to socialism seeks not to elide this confrontation, but to make it possible. To replace capitalism with socialism, writes Blanc, "(a) socialists should fight to win a socialist universal suffrage electoral majority in government/parliament and (b) socialists must expect that serious anti-capitalist change will necessarily require extra-parliamentary mass action like a general strike and a revolution to defeat the inevitable sabotage and resistance of the ruling class."

Though socialists are likely to be met with capitalist resistance that at times will turn violent, "revolution" doesn't necessitate mass bloodshed—and though we believe in self-defense, we certainly do not advocate violent means. A future socialist government, the late Marxist thinker Ralph Miliband wrote, "has only one major resource, namely its popular support." To pull off a revolution in our circumstances, that popular support would need to be mobilized both inside and outside of government.

Adherents of the democratic road strategy don't claim to know the precise sequence of events that will lead us to socialism, nor do we pretend it will be a cakewalk to eliminate capitalism, even with our people in power. Past attempts to make such transformations in countries like Chile and France have been stymied, as we'll get to later in this chapter. But we do know that the United States will not be able to achieve anything like socialist governance, and join other nations in the project of building international socialism, without both a mass movement of workers and the formal power to stop capitalists from undermining that movement as it engages in class struggle. We see engagement in electoral politics as an important tactic for accomplishing both of these goals, and ultimately bringing about a scenario in which the working class can actually win.

We've seen that left elected officials can not only win office, but can widen the scope of political possibility even when they're only a small minority of legislators in a given elected body. For a socialist movement that's been in the wilderness for at least half a century, these new developments are crucial. But it's not enough for socialists to be a tiny minority in the House of Representatives, or run inspiring but failed campaigns for president, or hold only 10 percent of seats in a city council. Our aims have to be much bigger than that. We don't want simply to fight against some other political majority—we want to *become* the majority, and believe we can get there.

Once we do, we will have to think very seriously about what our program should look like and how we will fight the capitalist backlash that will follow. If we aren't prepared for it, we're doomed to fail.

A note before we move on: the state itself boasts many stubborn, counter-majoritarian, antidemocratic practices, rules, and institutions that work in capitalists' favor, which have not only stymied the will of the majority of citizens repeatedly throughout American history, but also made many of those citizens pessimistic and dejected about the possibilities of politics making their lives better. A democratic socialist administration would therefore need to aggressively implement democratic reforms and work to rebuild average people's political confidence. Without such reforms, anything else we pursue will eventually meet formidable, possibly insurmountable obstacles. And without that sense of confidence in their ability to change the world, average people won't feel like joining a "political revolution" will amount to anything.

We don't have to wait until our state has been thoroughly transformed—until there is no more Citizens United, no gerrymandering, no voter suppression, no ballot line restrictions, no lifetime court appointments, no filibuster, no Electoral College, no Senate—before we can agitate around universal programs. But we also can't neglect the effort to reform the state itself. These projects should be pursued in tandem.

In our efforts to realize democratic reforms, we should remember that democratic rights are not benevolently handed down from above. They are won through struggle by average people, and they are met with protests and attempts at sabotage and repression from those who hold power. Winning a more democratic state will be just as difficult as winning better economic and social policies—and just as necessary.

Winning and Losing

The history of the Left around the world is filled with examples of socialists who have won only to lose. Take François Mitterrand, whose socialist government took power in France in 1981 on a platform that *Jacobin* founder and editor Bhaskar Sunkara calls "the most radical from a mainstream party in decades": it included public works programs, social housing, nurseries, clinics, expansion of union rights, increases in pensions and the minimum wage, nationalizations of major industries, and more. That program was met with a surge of enthusiasm; tens of thousands gathered at the Place de la Bastille in Paris the night the election results were announced.

Jonah Birch writes that Mitterrand's election "inspired a widespread belief that France was headed for a radical break with capitalism"—probably because the president made statements like, "You can be a manager of capitalist society or a founder of a socialist society. As far as we're concerned, we want to be the second." He also promised a "rupture" with capitalism and the beginnings of a "French road to socialism," and was reported to have said, "In economics, there are two solutions. Either you are a Leninist. Or you won't change anything."

But the business backlash was swift and intense. Capital flight soon pulled $5 billion in investment from the country, throwing Mitterrand's government into crisis. He soon backed off his bold proposals; by the end of his time in office in 1995, he couldn't even claim he had carried out a program of moderate reforms, much less put France on the road to socialism.

"Mitterrand had no interest in mobilizing a popular base to support his policy agenda; he surrounded himself with advisers who counseled restraint and retreat at every turn," Birch writes. "And he consistently sought to avoid exacerbating social and political tensions. That's unfortunate, because only through the kinds of measures and mobilizations that would inevitably provoke intensified conflicts with elites could the president hope to salvage his economic program."

The socialist promise of Mitterrand's administration quietly faded into oblivion. In Chile in 1973, Salvador Allende's was violently wrenched from his hands. Allende had been elected president of Chile in 1970 as part of the Popular Unity coalition of leftist parties. He immediately set out to democratically upend the Chilean order and move toward what some called a Chilean road to socialism. Allende's government nationalized the copper mines, Chile's most important industry and the site of huge profits for American mining companies, without compensation to their previous owners and investors. He increased workers' wages and reformed key sectors like health care and education in favor of working people.

Allende told the Chilean people that he didn't want simply "to improve and maintain the regime and the system," but "to change the regime and system and construct a new society on a completely different social and economic foundation." His election allowed for an expansion of the possible horizons envisioned by the Chilean people, as the historian Marian Schlotterbeck writes in *Beyond the Vanguard: Everyday Revolutionaries in Allende's Chile*, "enabl[ing] many Chileans to imagine revolutions beyond the promises of the Popular Unity platform."

Throughout that time, Allende faced vicious pushback from forces both domestic and foreign. Through the Central Intelligence Agency, the United States provided weapons and support for a failed attempt to overthrow his government in 1970 that killed the Chilean army's commander in chief, then helped provide a safe exit from the country for those behind the attempted coup. President Richard Nixon infamously demanded that the United States "make the economy scream" in Chile. When the Popular Unity coalition made significant gains in the March 1973 election, Ralph Miliband writes,

> The Right then understood that the electoral way was exhausted and that the way which remained [for them to fight the socialists] was that of force . . . So long as the Chilean Right believed that the experience of Popular Unity would come to an end by the will of the electors, it maintained a democratic attitude . . . When the Right came to fear that it would not pass and that the play of liberal institutions would result in the maintenance of Salvador Allende in power and in the development of social-ism, it preferred violence to the law.

The Chilean military, with the support of the American CIA, violently overthrew the Allende government in a coup on

September 11, 1973. As the coup unfolded, Allende either committed suicide or was killed, but not before giving a final radio address as the presidential palace was bombarded. "I will pay for loyalty to the people with my life," he said. "And I say to them that I am certain that the seed which we have planted in the good conscience of thousands and thousands of Chileans will not be shriveled forever."

The overthrow of Allende shows that domestic reactionary elements—the Chilean military, Chilean capital—as well as US imperialist forces through agencies like the CIA and elected leaders are more than willing to go beyond the bounds of democracy to stop a democratic socialist revolution in its tracks.

Bring It On

No one can claim to know exactly how those devastating defeats could have been avoided. "As a matter of general principle," Miliband once wrote about the Chilean coup, "one should be suspicious of people who have instant 'lessons' for every occasion. The chances are that they had them well before the occasion arose, and that they are merely trying to fit the experience to their prior views. So let us indeed be cautious about taking or giving 'lessons.'"

Still, it seems clear that one of the key missing ingredients in those failed attempts to transform Mitterrand's France or survive the violent overthrow of Allende's Chile was organized pressure from the working class itself. As Eric Blanc writes, "Avoiding the dead-end of social democratization will above all require a very intense and sustained degree of mass action and independent working-class organization outside of parliament. Without this, even the most well-intentioned government will flounder."

Socialists shouldn't despair at the histories of countries like Chile under Allende or France under Mitterrand, tragic though they are. These examples don't prove that future socialist efforts are doomed, but rather show some mistakes of our predecessors who have taken power—mistakes that we must do our best now to avoid. Foremost among them is the need to not shy away from stoking conflict between the working class that elected us and the capitalists who want to destroy us. If we are to take power, that conflict is inevitable; we have to figure out how to govern in such a way as to build up our own forces at the grassroots level. (We take up the question of how to do that in the next chapter.)

We can't just elect our way to a better world. We have to build a bottom-up movement that can change the conditions in which elected officials make decisions, and force policies that benefit the vast majority of people and the planet. Once we've built such a movement and won successes at the ballot box, that movement will have to defend its gains and its very existence against hostile capitalists with enormous power to stop them.

The Phantom Limb

Figuring out what socialist strategy in the United States should look like, especially electoral strategy, as part of a democratic road to socialism requires wrestling with some of our country's eccentricities. One distinct feature of our political system that makes things a lot harder for socialists is our lack of a genuine, mass left-wing party of any kind. Instead of a workers' or socialist party, we're stuck with the Democrats.

More and more people are coming to the realization that the Democratic Party really sucks. That has a lot to do with the fact that it is a fundamentally capitalist party—and one that's not even a real party, in the sense of having a meaningful definition of membership, robust internal mechanisms that allow members to determine the party's agenda, or an ability to discipline its candidates who don't carry out that democratically agreed-upon agenda, as the parties of most other countries around the world do.

For nearly all of the past century, those fighting for progressive social change have mainly faced two choices, neither of them ideal: operate in the electoral realm as Democrats because there is no other game in town, or (with a few notable exceptions) remain doomed to complete electoral irrelevance. Sociologist Barry Eidlin calls our "missing labor party . . . a 'phantom limb' of American politics, an amputation of the political spectrum whose pain is still felt in its absence."

Among political journalists and average Americans, the typical political shorthand is that the Democrats are the party of the people and the Republicans are the party of big business. But the truth is a lot more complicated. Organized labor, antiracists, feminists, environmentalists, social democrats, socialists, and others have long operated within the Democratic Party. But that doesn't mean it's their party.

While these groups hold varying degrees of power within the party, and most are seen as key constituencies to keep happy as part of the party base, they aren't the ones ultimately calling the shots. Wall Street and the financial sector, real estate developers, Silicon Valley tech companies, media and entertainment executives—these are the wealthy donors and power players that usually get their way within the party. Progressive forces are an important part of the party's coalition, and they've sometimes been able to compel the party to move on a more left-wing agenda. But, historically, progressives' interests have usually been subordinate to these sectors of capital—and primarily accommodated when they pose no substantive threat to capital.

This contrasts sharply to most other comparable countries in the world, which have labor or socialist parties that don't have such deep ties to capital. The presence of such parties in those countries makes their politics far different. Take Canada, for example, a country similar to our own that Eidlin argues is useful for comparative purposes. Canada has a social democratic party, the New Democratic Party, that is the major third party in the country's politics. (The other two parties are a right-wing party, the Conservative Party, and a center-left party, the Liberals.) Though it has held significant seats in parliament and the leadership of some provinces, no NDP candidate has ever won the prime ministership of Canada. The NDP was the official opposition party—which, in the Canadian case, usually means the party with the second-largest party in government—only once, in 2011.

Yet despite rarely holding official power on the national level, Eidlin argues that the NDP has played a key role in advancing pro-worker reforms in Canada, like establishing the country's national health system and supporting the Canadian labor movement. Like most social democratic parties around the world, the NDP has moved rightward in recent decades; some leaders have argued that such a move and an abandonment of a robust working-class agenda would lead to electoral breakthroughs. (They've usually been proven very wrong, whether in the short term or long term.) But because the party has structural ties to the labor movement and does not have the kinds of deep ties to Canadian capital that the Democrats have in the United States, it has been able to fight harder for workers and play a key role in building and defending the Canadian welfare state.

In the United States, pro-labor policies are often viewed as a bone thrown to a "special interest group" such as unions or other organizations representing discrete sections of the working class—no different from policies implemented to curry favor with, say, organized groups of motel owners, or the National Rifle Association. But in Canada, the NDP has been able to shape the political landscape such that pro-labor policies are seen as broadly beneficial to the Canadian working class, and indeed all of Canadian society.

A former strategist for Richard Nixon once described the Democratic Party as "history's second-most enthusiastic capitalist party." This holds up. Major industries wouldn't drown the party in donations if they didn't feel the Democrats were capable of or willing to protect their financial interests. And drown it they do.

In the 2018 midterms, for example, the industry that contributed the most money to US elections was the securities and investments industry, which is dominated by Wall Street firms. Groups and individuals representing that industry spent over $400 million to bankroll candidates and secure electoral outcomes it found favorable. If you assumed the majority of that money went to Republicans, you'd be wrong. A slim majority actually went to Democrats.

A look at donations from individual organizations shows how the game is played. Take the National Association of Realtors, the real estate industry's top lobbying group, which contributed over $2 million to political campaigns and PACs in 2019. The group split its contributions almost perfectly evenly between Republicans and Democrats. The National Association of Realtors doesn't care which party is in power—it just wants to make sure the financial interests of its own power players are catered to at the end of the day. The purpose of political donations is to curry favor with potential victors. It's also an implicit threat: our money helped you get where you are, and if we decide to take it away, there's no guarantee your political career will survive.

If socialists and progressives want to stand a chance at winning office and implementing reform that will hurt capitalists' bottom line as it empowers everybody else, we are for the moment largely forced to share a party with our own opponents. In the 2018 elections, a group called Euclidean Capital, run by hedge fund billionaire James Simons, gave $16 million to push Democrats over the finish line, mainly contributing to Democratic Party super PACs that, unlike individual campaigns, can absorb unlimited amounts of money. When progressive Democrats fight to tax Wall Street to offset public spending on education, housing, health care, and a clean environment for ordinary working-class people, they're actually fighting *against* powerful people and organizations that are bankrolling their own party. And the playing field is not tilted in their favor.

This contradiction is why socialists believe that to really go toe-to-toe with the capitalist class, we're eventually going to have to create a party that doesn't make any room for Euclidean Capital or the National Association of Realtors—a party that's explicitly dedicated to advancing the interests of the working class and acting contrary to the interests of the capitalist class (and a party led by people who know that the interests of these classes are mutually exclusive). The lack of such a party in the United States is a major reason why it has such a weak social welfare state in comparison with other countries, as well as a political culture that until very recently didn't see any critique of capitalism as an acceptable part of the discourse.

Structural Barriers

Why don't we just create an independent workers' party, then? Ah, if only it were that simple.

Many Americans believe that the US two-party system isn't serving their needs. A 2019 NBC/*Wall Street Journal* poll found 38 percent of Americans believed we need a third party; a Gallup poll the year before found 57 percent had that opinion. If there were a credible political alternative out there, many people would probably vote for it. The problem is that there are enormous structural barriers in the United States to forming such a party.

To start with, we have a winner-take-all, first-past-the-post electoral system rather than a proportional representation system. We also have what *Jacobin* editor Seth Ackerman calls "a unique—and uniquely repressive—legal system governing political parties and the mechanics of elections." This includes absurdly high requirements for the number of votes required to get on the ballot for a party's nomination and all but infinite opportunities for the parties themselves to destroy any third-party challengers—barriers that do not exist in any other democracy around the world.

"Today, in almost every established democracy, getting on the ballot is at most a secondary concern for small or new parties; in many countries it involves little more than filling out some forms," Ackerman writes. Not so in the land of the free: indeed, "some US electoral procedures are unknown outside of dictatorships."

Even if a third party does somehow manage to muscle its way onto the ballot, staying there is incredibly onerous and deeply distracting. This is in part why Bernie Sanders left the Liberty Union Party. In his 1977 resignation letter, he said that he felt that the organization was narrowly focused on preparing itself for and conducting electoral campaigns, each one an uphill battle.

This wasn't entirely the party's own fault—the amount of work required to keep a third party in the game detracts from the kind of year-round organizing it takes to actually build a base that can put it over the top, such as being directly involved in community and labor activism to gain the trust of the working class and its institutions, building and contributing to independent media to reshape the political narrative, doing political education and practicing internal democracy in the party itself to train members and increase their capacity, and so on.

And the already existing barriers often become even more difficult if the major parties sense a third party could become a challenge to them. If a third party's star starts to rise in a particular state, for example, the major parties may use their advantage to pass legislation to restrict ballot access or throw up other hurdles to suppress the threat. The result is that third parties that are able to navigate the obstacle course and build a following can become victims of their own success.

This happened to the Libertarian Party in Arizona in 2015. The GOP-dominated legislature, worried about libertarians nipping at their heels, increased the signature requirements for a candidate to appear on a party's primary ballot from 134 to 3,023. That's on top of the onerous requirements for that party to appear on the ballot line in Arizona in the first place. Republicans, who were far better resourced, wouldn't have a hard time meeting the new requirements. Libertarians, who lacked the resources of their Republican opponents but still posed a threat to them by splitting conservative votes and thus benefiting Democrats, would. A Republican state legislator helpfully summed up why his party sought the legal change:

"I believe that, if you look at the last election, there was at least one, probably two, congressional seats that may have gone in a different direction, the direction I would have liked to have seen them go, if this requirement had been there."

There are other problems, too. Pro-worker third parties ironically have a hard time attracting the support of labor unions, even though since the beginning of the neoliberal onslaught against the US labor movement unions' political influence through the Democrats has declined. Rather than form another party altogether, they've remained in the Democratic Party coalition, and Democratic candidates still rely on them heavily for donations: American unions gave the party at least $157 million in the 2016 cycle. Even despite these truckloads of cash, we've seen a dramatic decline in unions' ability or willingness to assert themselves politically, to push the party to fight for pro-worker and pro-union policies and legal reforms. Union leaders aren't seeing many fruits from their strategy of standing steadfastly by the Democrats and handing over massive amounts of their members' dues to the party—a strategy that, as labor scholar Kim Moody has noted, is actively detrimental to union programs like organizing new workers—yet they seem uninterested in changing it.

With union leaders sticking to this failing strategy, it's hard enough to get them to endorse progressive challengers *within* the Democratic Party if their odds don't look good, even when those challengers are clearly more oriented to the working class and unions themselves. Nearly all the major unions endorsed Hillary Clinton over Bernie Sanders in 2016, despite the fact that Sanders was the most pro-labor presidential candidate in living memory. Getting unions to ally with progressive challengers *outside* the Democratic Party is even harder.

For example, the Labor Party, formed in 1996, was an earnest and laudable attempt to form an independent workers' party in the United States. It sought to pull the labor movement's support away from the Democratic Party, given how constantly it threw labor under the bus to appease the capitalist portion of its base whose interests were diametrically opposed to those of the labor movement. But despite being explicitly set up for that purpose, the Labor Party failed to attract the support of labor unions themselves.

The party's socialist founder, Tony Mazzocchi, said in 1996 that he'd "never found a person in the top labor leadership say they're opposed to a labor party." So Mazzocchi and other activists built it—and yet, wary of alienating Democratic Party top brass and considering the risk too great, those labor leaders didn't come. Neither did union members, for the most part.

The Labor Party had a phenomenal platform, ambitious and attractive. But without mass support, the party feared being branded as spoilers—a common problem for third parties and indeed one of the reasons the Green Party's popular support is diminished—so they declined to run candidates. A noble effort led by some of the brightest and most committed socialists and progressives of the era, the Labor Party fizzled out in less than a decade.

An intended result of the two-party stranglehold is to keep left-wing challenges to two-party hegemony out of the running. Anyone making a serious effort to build an independent third party risks marginalization, either by coming off as a spoiler and actively alienating allies, or by laying low in an attempt to not come off as a spoiler and failing to attract allies. Similarly, third parties often either expend all their political energy and capacity in pursuit of ballot line access and visibility, like the Green Party, or conclude that they can't contest for power without an independent ballot line and so forgo the opportunity to mount meaningful challenges, like the Labor Party. In view of these options, many activists decide it's better to just hold their nose and engage with the Democratic Party, or to eschew electoral politics entirely. And that's precisely the outcome the system is designed to achieve.

This should make us all extremely angry. The United States purports to be a democratic country, yet our laws and rules governing the creation of new parties are seemingly insurmountable. "The two-party system has long been brain dead—kept alive by support systems like state electoral laws that protect the established parties from rivals and by federal subsidies and so-called campaign reform," political scientist Theodore Lowi wrote in 1992. It "would collapse in an instant if the tubes were pulled and the IVs were cut," but we can't seem to take it off life support.

Realignment Blues

Because of these structural barriers to creating a new party, many American leftists have tried to turn the Democratic Party into a working-class party over the past half-century. This has been called the "realignment strategy," because the aim is to realign the Democrats from a pro-capitalist party with important working-class and progressive constituencies to an actually working-class, progressive party—moving those two constituencies from being junior partners to the ones calling the shots, and pushing the reactionary elements out of the party.

Proponents of the realignment strategy have made important gains on this front in the last half-century that shouldn't be dismissed. In some key aspects, they have succeeded. But unfortunately, as sociologist Paul Heideman has written, the ultimate goal of turning the Democrats into a workers' party has failed.

In the 1960s, the civil rights movement and Students for a Democratic Society set out to drive Southern white supremacists out of the Democratic coalition. These racists were long a part of the Democratic coalition, and they often sided with sectors of capital against other elements of the Democratic Party coalition—particularly African Americans—to thwart the agenda of the party's left wing. The Dixiecrats prevented the New Deal from achieving all the progressive gains it could have, and continued to wield a disproportionate amount of power within the party relative to their numbers for decades afterward. Getting rid of this reactionary rump was a key task if the Democrats were ever going to become a workers' party.

Cleveland Sellers, an organizer in the Student Nonviolent Coordinating Committee and Mississippi Freedom Democratic Party, wrote about the civil rights movement's strategy: "Our ultimate goal was the destruction of the awesome power of the Dixiecrats, who controlled over 75 percent of the most important committees in Congress. With the Dixiecrats deposed, the way would have been clear for a wide-ranging redistribution of wealth, power, and priorities throughout the nation."

Those students and civil rights activists were ultimately successful in driving white racists out of the party. The passage of the Civil Rights Act in 1964, the end of Jim Crow, and the political transformation of African Americans from an excluded group of second-class citizens who lacked even the right to vote in the South to a key part of the Democratic Party's constituency drove the Southern white supremacists into the arms of the Republican Party, where they and their racist political descendants still are today.

This is an incredible moral and political achievement, one of the most monumental in all of American history. No one should downplay its significance today. But the goal of fundamentally realigning the party toward the working class and driving out the anti-labor elements of the party remained out of reach.

White supremacists exited the Democratic coalition, but the Democrats weren't transformed into the party of the working class that Sellers and other organizers had hoped for. In fact, the party soon went in the opposite direction, drifting rightward on key economic issues, abandoning the working class in favor of corporate-friendly free trade agreements, refusing to fight back against vicious union-busting, and joining in the dismantling of America's already meager welfare state. That's because while the racist Dixiecrats were expelled from the coalition, key sectors of capital remained, and their money gave them considerable power. By dangling donations, lobbying, funding think tanks, rooting themselves in the elite institutions where party operatives were trained, and threatening to wreak havoc on the economy if they didn't get their way, the capitalist elements of the Democratic Party coalition helped guide the party into the embrace of neoliberalism.

Into the 1980s and '90s, major Democratic figures like Bill Clinton carried out devastating anti-worker policies, including the plan to "end welfare as we know it," the destruction of huge swaths of the nation's public housing stock, and ramping up the war on drugs and mass incarceration—policies that disproportionately affected black Americans. Clinton even occasionally made racist symbolic gestures a key part of his campaigning, like announcing his "tough on crime" agenda at Stone Mountain, a Georgia monument to white supremacy, while standing in front of a group of nearly all-black prisoners—their appearance resembling a Jim Crow–era chain gang—in 1992. Likewise, Hillary Clinton used the dehumanizing neologism "superpredators" to describe young black people in 1996 while arguing for tougher policing and harsher sentencing. The open white supremacists were gone from the party, but the party couldn't even be counted on as a steadfast ally in the fight against racism, much less fight for the working class.

In the wake of the civil rights movement, Michael Harrington, who cofounded the Democratic Socialists of America and was the most prominent socialist in the United States until his death in 1989, continued to push to realign the Democratic Party. But with an economic crisis, the flight of important sectors of capital like oil from the Democrats to the Republicans (which helped leave the Democrats vulnerable to new attacks from other segments of capital), and a decline in labor militancy beginning in the 1970s, he and his coalition of socialists, the left wing of the labor movement, and other progressives weren't able to make much headway. Paul Heideman writes,

> The contradiction between the party's base and its investors has existed since the birth of the modern Democratic Party in the New Deal. It has persisted through the Great Society, through the New Politics era, through Carter, all the way up until the present. Again and again, this contradiction alone has proven inert, unable to change the basic structure of power within the party.

The Dirty Break

Let's recap this depressing history: the Democrats have long been beholden to the capitalist class, and to build a working-class political alternative we need to break with them. Many have tried to do so in the past, but the structural barriers to doing so are incredibly high. Realizing this, leftists and other progressive organizers have attempted to transform the Democrats and push out the reactionary elements within the party rather than form a new one. While they had some important successes, the party is further to the right on many key issues than ever before. Bleak.

But all hope is not lost. Enter what Eric Blanc has called a "dirty break" strategy.

To explain the dirty break strategy, it's helpful to first explain the "clean break" strategy it's responding to. The argument for a clean break is that the only way to break with the Democratic Party is to withdraw support for all its candidates and immediately build a true left-wing political alternative outside the two-party system. Adherents to this strategy, while few and far between these days, are vocal and worth responding to. Their justification for a clean break is rooted in the territory we just covered: we need a party of our own, and the realignment strategy has proven a failure.

The clean breakers are not totally wrong—we do need such a party, and realignment has failed. But they neglect to mention that their strategy has been a complete failure, too. Despite decades of leftist exhortations to break with the Democrats and build a party of the working class, and occasionally noble but doomed efforts to use the Green Party or other leftist third parties to carry out that break, we haven't made any headway in this regard. As critics of the clean break strategy sometimes say, it's not a party until there's a crowd, and we definitely don't have a real crowd around the Greens or any other third party. It's not as easy as "Build it and they will come."

The failures of that strategy lead us to the dirty break, which is honest about both the fundamental need to break with the Democrats and the serious structural barriers to doing so. The strategy aims to go beyond the two-party system by going through it. We can use the Democratic Party ballot line strategically, for our own purposes: to wage campaigns that heighten the level of class consciousness in society, encourage people to take militant action in the form of strikes and other kinds of protest activity, and even raise awareness of and interest in socialism.

In the meantime, we can sharpen the contradictions between the Democratic base—the working-class and generally progressive rank-and-file members of the party—and the wealthy Democratic Party funders who don't want anything to do with the base's demands. "Rather than yet another suicidal frontal assault" on the Democrats—the clean break— "we need to mount the electoral equivalent of guerrilla insurgency," Ackerman writes. The idea is to agitate within the party, in full view of the party's base, in order to engage as many people in the discussion as possible, making it harder to ignore. As conflicts between the base and the funders grow, the aim is to build up and cohere a powerful working-class pole, whose growing strength will eventually pose the practical question of a split with the Democrats and the creation of a party of our own.

Parts of this strategy may sound familiar: the agitational elements resemble the way Sanders's campaigns have played out within the Democratic Party. He is a long-standing independent, one of the few in Congress, who has spoken throughout his career of the need for working people to have a party of their own. Writing of the previously mentioned Labor Party in 1997, Sanders commented on the party's slogan: "'The bosses have two parties. We need one of our own.' Hard to argue with that."

But, in order to continually be elected to the congressional positions he has held, he has also figured out a working relationship with the Vermont Democratic Party. In order to work in Congress, he has done much the same with Democrats there. And, of course, he has run for president twice as a Democrat.

Sanders and several of his key aides have spoken often about the need to remake the Democratic Party. As proponents of the dirty break strategy, we advise against that—no need to confuse people about the party's redeemability. Still, whether he would cop to it or not, much of Sanders's strategy is very similar to what we're arguing for. And unlike the leftists over the years who have insisted on the danger and futility of ever engaging with the Democrats in any way, Sanders's campaign sparked a movement at both the electoral and non-electoral levels for more working-class militancy, more interest in socialism and the socialist movement, and, perhaps just as important, more disillusionment with the Democratic Party.

Sanders's presidential campaigns, and the campaigns that have followed like Ocasio-Cortez's, have gone up against the power brokers of the Democratic Party. Their conflicts haven't been limited to their direct opponents: Sanders tussled with Democratic National Committee in 2016, and Ocasio-Cortez has sparred with House Majority Leader Nancy Pelosi, beginning on her very first day in office when she joined a sit-in for the Green New Deal in Pelosi's office. Especially for young people, many of whom are getting interested and involved in politics for the first time, these intra-party conflicts have been eye-opening, revealing how the Democratic power brokers will move heaven and earth to defeat even mildly progressive demands on the party. Observers of these conflicts increasingly find themselves asking, *What kind of a "progressive" party is this? Who does it really fight for: the many, or the few?*

To be sure, despite his long history of arguing for the need for a new party for working people, since his 2016 campaign, Sanders has emphasized the need to remake the Democratic Party, not break with it. Similarly, Ocasio-Cortez has never argued for the need to fully break with the Democrats (though, crucially, she has emphasized that the Democrats are not a true left party and said that in any other country, she and centrists like Joe Biden wouldn't be in the same party). But again, her orientation checks many of the boxes that dirty-break adherents would argue for. Whereas historically those pursuing the realignment strategy have explicitly collaborated with some wings of the Democratic Party establishment against others, Sanders and Ocasio-Cortez are more given to broad anti-establishment agitation, which creates a different and more dirty break–friendly dynamic. Their efforts to heighten the class contradictions within the Democratic Party may even help lead us down a path that can culminate with a real break with the Democrats in the long term, intended or not.

We can't rely on individuals like Sanders and Ocasio-Cortez to wage a dirty-break fight on their own. As steadfastly righteous and principled as someone like Sanders may be, to build a movement that is much larger than him we need an organization that can coordinate our candidates and elected officials and hold them accountable to a left-wing program.

Ackerman argues that we need something like a party, but emphasizes that a party doesn't have to be defined by whether or not its name appears on a ballot. Instead, a party can simply be a democratic organization with internal education, a democratically decided platform, candidates who run on whatever ballot line (one that is Democratic or independent when it makes sense, or even, theoretically, Republican if that somehow makes sense), and the ability and willingness to discipline its candidates and elected officials if they stop adhering to the party's program. This would get us closer to the way real parties function; it's also a way for us to stop worrying about whether or not we should run as Democrats or not, and instead focus on building an organization that can get our people elected and build necessary non-electoral movements at the same time. This is the role that a group like the Democratic Socialists of America can play and has played in its rebirth over the last few years: not running candidates on a DSA ballot line yet, but acting as something like a party for the candidates it does run, and for the rest of its members as well.

The tricky part, of course, is figuring out how to use all this energy to actually split from the Democrats someday—to "break" with the Dems after getting "dirtied" by running as Democrats. Nobody has a full blueprint for how to do this (though Blanc cites some historical examples like the Minnesota Farmer-Labor Party that can give us clues). But in the short term, building up our forces and raising popular expectations while drawing out the differences between the working-class Democratic base and capitalist-funded Democratic establishment, is the way forward.

Right now, there are a few electorally focused organizations heightening these contradictions by running progressive challengers, including ones that are not explicitly socialist—such as Justice Democrats, which like DSA backed Ocasio-Cortez and has retained close ties with her. But socialist organizations like DSA have some unique advantages.

Socialist Organizations

DSA has exploded in size since 2016, and many of the ideas and policy proposals advanced by the organization have moved from marginal to mainstream in an incredibly short period. That development is invaluable. But the organization's long-term impact on American politics could be even greater: DSA can be the motor driving forward the dirty-break strategy, and even potentially the kernel of a new party.

This is a big claim, of course, and whether or not it comes to pass will depend on innumerable factors—some of which we can control, some that are beyond our control, some that we can't even foresee. But in the few short years since the organization's rebirth, it has shown signs that it's capable of acting much like the kind of party that Ackerman argues for. Though the organization's big-tent approach to leftist organizing means that what its members think and do are not consistent throughout the country, it does provide basic socialist political education and organizational training to its active members. DSA doesn't have a completely thought-out method for disciplining its electoral candidates, but has taken steps in the right direction.

For example, in 2018, after Ocasio-Cortez told CNN that she "look[s] forward to . . . us rallying behind all Democratic nominees, including the governor"—Andrew Cuomo, a neoliberal Democrat who is exactly the kind of elected official DSA exists to fight—"to make sure that he wins in November," New York City DSA released a statement reiterating their support for Ocasio-Cortez and noting the historic nature of her campaign, but also criticizing her statement about the governor. Socialists "have a responsibility to name our enemies, and high on that list is Andrew Cuomo," the letter said, explaining that "rallying behind all Democratic nominees' erases the real distance between insurgent socialist candidates and the Democratic Party establishment that we must continue to fight against." To her credit, rather than pull away from DSA after being publicly chided, OcasioCortez hosted a DSA-members-only town hall in Queens a month after the statement, having come there directly from an appearance on the late-night show *Jimmy Kimmel Live!* alongside rapper Cardi B, swapping a TV studio for a dingy community center where she fielded questions from socialists for two hours.

At the 2019 national DSA convention in Atlanta (to which we were both elected delegates), the organization took further steps in this direction. In addition to passing a resolution calling for a class-struggle electoral strategy, the organization voted to back only Bernie Sanders in the 2020 presidential race. The reasoning was to abandon a "lesser evil" approach to endorsing a presidential candidate and instead take an uncompromising stance on what a DSA-endorsed candidate should look like.

This is a move that could bring the organization closer to something resembling a socialist party. In the Democratic Party orbit are an endless number of progressive pressure groups, which decide on their endorsements by adding up who's got the best platform and record, who's most likely to win, and who's made flattering overtures or promised future access to the group itself. An organization that aspires to behave like its own party can't follow their lead. While a socialist party would ideally run its own candidates, it should at the very least only back those candidates who explicitly advance a socialist agenda—and be content to withhold endorsement in the event that no such candidate is running.

One difficulty in keeping successful electoral candidates faithful to a DSA platform and vision is that, because the organization is so young, few candidates are running for office who have organically emerged from DSA itself. There are exceptions to this, such as Julia Salazar's successful run for New York State Senate in 2018. While Salazar's emergence from DSA is no guarantee of her long-term fealty to a DSA political program, her first year in office, at the time of this writing, has been promising. But many of DSA's victorious candidates haven't come directly from its own ranks. Instead, while they are members of DSA and the organization played a critical role in getting them elected, they cut their teeth elsewhere, in unions, community groups, and racial justice groups.

A successful socialist organization, and certainly one that hopes to be the seed of a future party, will always have to work closely with other progressive groups as long as they're on board with a class-struggle program—otherwise, it will be doomed to sectarian irrelevance like so many previous party-building attempts. That said, producing true DSA candidates who are steeped in the organization's political program and have proven themselves dedicated socialist organizers is something to aspire to.

The future of DSA is unknown, of course. The organization could fizzle, or collapse, or get absorbed into the Democratic Party apparatus. We have faith in DSA and think these outcomes are improbable in the short term, but they are possible. But even if DSA itself isn't the ultimate organizational vehicle for a new left-wing political party in American life, it could be training a generation of people who will go on to form that party. Currently, it's the best hope we have—and a good one at that.

The Necessity of a Political Vision

Socialist groups bring something particular and necessary to the fight for the world that we want to live in. The goal of socialism is enormous, epochal in scale: it's to consciously reshape our political and economic system in a way that benefits all people, not just a privileged and wealthy few. This has never been successfully carried out in world history. We can't accomplish such a massive task haphazardly, or expect the solutions to fall into our lap. We need a plan, and an army. A socialist group can help generate that plan and build that army in a way that no other formation can.

Political education is something a socialist organization is uniquely equipped to do on a large scale. The history of socialism and the ideas that animate it aren't taught in schools or talked about in the corporate media. When a person's curiosity about socialism is piqued, they do have some independent media options that can help them get a handle on socialism (that's what our own magazine, *Jacobin*, and our publisher, Verso, aim to do). But there's no substitute for the kind of deep political education that an active and dynamic socialist group can offer.

DSA, which was fortunate enough to absorb all the new socialist energy coming out of the first Sanders campaign, mixes political education with action. Across the country, DSA chapters are engaged in campaigns of their members' own devising, decisions arrived at by democratic debate on the local and national level. Political education helps elucidate the history of various strategies and assists organizers in assessing the strengths and weaknesses of the work they're already doing on the ground. Study, then, enhances collective action.

A few years into our time in DSA, a funny thing began to happen to us. People long active in the socialist movement would inquire where and by whom DSA members were trained in theory and analysis before joining DSA. They couldn't believe that people new to the scene, people who had no prior experience or education, could hold their own in conversations about Marxist analysis, previously the exclusive domain of small, disciplined socialist groups. We told them the truth: the heavy emphasis on action in DSA has given a sense of urgency to the project of political education, and that urgency has sharpened and clarified our political analysis.

DSA members have been reading and studying to make sense of the work they're already engaged in and figure out what to do next. (In case you haven't picked up on it yet, that is also what we would like you, the reader, to do with this book.) The enormous amount of organizing work undertaken by DSA in the last few years has posed questions with real stakes, and political education has been a tool for figuring out how to act in the moment. That dynamic relationship between education and real-world organizing has accelerated DSA members' political development.

Many people are hard at work fighting one or another expression of capitalism. But without a socialist organization, they can fail to situate their own fight in the broader theoretical and historical context. That means that when faced with urgent questions, they will often come to wrong conclusions and unknowingly repeat mistakes from the past. On the other hand, there are leftists who are only tenuously connected to real, concrete struggles against capitalism, whose political education becomes a stale exercise in the isolated preservation of a tradition—useful for keeping socialist ideas in circulation but vulnerable to them becoming rigid orthodoxy. Only an organization that is engaged in both intensive organizing work and socialist political education can square the circle.

Socialists need to learn about the history of our movement and its ideas and strategies not only from books but from real, living people. Where else can a young radical meet older socialists who have tried things before, sometimes with success and other times with failure, than in a socialist organization?

In DSA we have been fortunate enough to meet people who live in our own cities who we may never have met otherwise—people who were members of Students for a Democratic Society, people with experience building independent third parties, people who took rank-and-file union jobs in the seventies (in an application of the "rank-and-file strategy" that we discuss in Chapter 6) and have been attempting to build a democratic and militant labor movement ever since.

One of the major problems facing the new generation of socialists in the United States—most of whom are, like us, in their twenties and thirties—is that up to now, we haven't had mentors sharing with us the lessons they learned from their years in struggle. We will always suffer somewhat from this deficit: the number of socialists and the size and strength of socialist organizations facilitating that mentorship have dwindled in the last fifty years. This interruption has left many young radicals rudderless and trying to reinvent the wheel.

We now thankfully have a large and welcoming institution that can connect socialists across generations, uniting the few who kept the flame alive with the tens of thousands who are carrying the torch into the future. It's important that this institution is democratic, so that young socialists don't feel they are merely taking direction from those who came before them—an unappealing prospect for many people who already have a shitty boss and don't want another—but instead feel that they are learning and organizing among equals, some of whom have rich personal histories and valuable experiences.

Democratic Practice

Democracy is a vital component of any socialist organization. If cultivated and safeguarded in practice, it can transform an institution into a force to be reckoned with. In *Democracy Is Power: Rebuilding Unions from the Bottom Up* by Mike Parker and Martha Gruelle—two longtime socialists who come out of that rank-and-file tradition and are now members of DSA—the authors make the case for democracy in unions:

> Union power requires democracy. Unions need active members to be strong, and people won't stay involved for long if they don't have control of the union's program . . . Working people are fit to run our own affairs. We are intelligent, can act cooperatively, and are fully capable of analyzing our situation and crafting the best strategy to improve it. Given real choices we will overcome our prejudices and work for the betterment of all.

The same principles apply to socialist organizations. The reasons for prioritizing democracy are both defensive and offensive. Having democratic structures and a culture of democratic deliberation gives members a sense of ownership over the organization and is our best bet to keep people engaged for the long haul. A democratic organization of socialists can be like a democratic union, teaching members how to think critically and cooperate, and even preparing them to govern a future society in which they are in charge.

By "democratic structures," we mean having rules that apply equally to everyone, having transparency about what those rules are and how they work, and striking a balance between majoritarian decision-making (if the membership votes to do something, that's what happens) and the protection of political minorities (people who don't agree with the majority are free to express their dissent and organize around an alternate vision). By "a culture of democratic deliberation," we mean establishing a norm of elevating disagreements from the personal level to the political level, openly arguing for our ideas, and responding with grace when those ideas are defeated. There are very few places in the United States where ordinary people get to actually practice democracy in this way. That's why, at first, people coming into a democratic organization may be startled by being forced to hash out disagreements. But over time, people learn to cooperate, build coalitions, and organize to win people over to their ideas instead of shouting down their opposition. These are precisely the political skills with which we need to maneuver in the world outside our socialist organizations.

Organizational democracy equips socialists with crucial leadership skills, too. Thousands of DSA members serve as leaders in local and national leadership bodies of the organization. Here, for the first time in their lives, they are handed political dilemmas that require great finesse and for which they are personally responsible, whether that's a fight within the organization that's impeding organizing work or an attack from outside that requires a well-calibrated response.

Thousands of socialists are therefore learning in real time how to demonstrate leadership in complex situations. They are learning through trial and error when to fall back and when to step out ahead, when to stand firm and when to admit they were wrong, and how to cultivate solidarity through their own actions as leaders. And they're learning critical administrative skills, too, from keeping proper records to managing group finances.

This is the stuff of governance. We can talk about wanting a socialist-run state, but we won't be prepared to handle it unless we practice democracy now, among ourselves.

Going Bigger

But a socialist organization isn't just about the people already in it. We need a mass movement. Political education in DSA therefore isn't just about equipping our current members with tools to enhance our own ability to strategize—it's also about training legions of organizers who can act as persuaders and translators, interpreting the miseries and crises that ordinary people face in a way that pulls them closer to socialist analysis.

It's important here to resist the allure of "vanguardism," an approach to organizing that sees ideologically committed socialists as possessors of a higher knowledge who bluntly impart that knowledge to the dumb working-class masses. In American socialist history, this has often resulted in tiny sects convinced of their leadership role yet leading no one, pumping out propaganda that nobody reads (and usually developing personalities that nobody wants to be around in the process). But while we can't just tell people what we think and expect them to listen, we also think our ideas can help transform the world. We want to make the case to people that the source of their problems is not themselves or each other, but the capitalist class and the capitalist system as a whole.

To avoid a dogmatism that would alienate others, our best bet is to stand alongside people in active struggle, whether that's for a better union contract or for Medicare for All, and to explain the shape and the stakes of the struggle as we understand them in real time, as equal participants in the fight. We can only build class consciousness on a mass scale by earnestly and devotedly pushing for working-class demands ourselves, and in the process earning trust from people who aren't yet socialists.

The socialist movement needs to be bigger—much bigger. It also needs to become more diverse and more reflective of the working class in this country. When McCarthyism purged radicals from the labor movement and large swaths of civic life, it severed the organic link that had previously existed between socialists and the working class. Many workers lost their only connection to the socialist tradition. Radicals, meanwhile, often retreated to the academy, one of the few places they weren't completely driven out of (though it certainly wasn't always safe for radicals and still isn't).

The long-term effects of this mid-century assault on working-class radicals are evident in the demographics of today's DSA, which is primarily white and largely made up of college-educated members (which isn't to say DSA members today are not wage workers—almost all are—or people of color). And since recruitment is often informal, with people making their way to the organization through their preexisting social networks, the demographics have been self-reproducing, even as DSA has ballooned in size.

To change this situation, again, the answer is outward-facing struggle. Organized socialists must wage deliberate campaigns to root us in the broader working class. Bernie Sanders's 2020 campaign offers a useful example—an August 2019 poll conducted by the Pew Research Center found that his base was the most working-class and least white of all the candidates for the Democratic Party presidential nomination. Other polls repeatedly confirmed that this was especially true among young people. Sanders has exposed millions of working-class people, including many working-class people of color (especially young people), to socialist ideas for the first time since at least the New Left era, if not earlier. DSA has campaigned for a Bernie Sanders victory in 2020 with a specific eye toward engaging young, working-class people of color who support Sanders—focusing efforts, for example, on community college organizing in cities like New York and the East Bay.

Unions, too, are important sites of organizing if DSA wants to diversify its base. Union members are all working-class by definition and disproportionately people of color; black workers are the most likely to be unionized of any racial group. And union fights against management are encounters where class consciousness is already percolating, and where solidarity is always welcome. DSA has launched numerous labor solidarity campaigns that bring socialist organizers into close working relationships with already-organized members of the multiracial working class—not as outsider evangelists, but as allies in struggles that are unfolding in real time. Labor solidarity campaigns hold great promise for bridging the racial and cultural gaps that exist between self-identified socialists and the rest of the working class.

The particular dilemmas of multiracial working-class organizing are important, but beyond the scope of this book. Suffice to say that given the current demographics of the movement, organized socialists have a responsibility to convince the most passionate and politicized members of the working class that if they are ready to join the fight for socialism, they can and should belong to a socialist organization. But no matter how strong our appeals, working-class people with little time and heavy burdens will not join if they have the perception that a socialist organization can't do anything for them. Socialist organizations must therefore, above all, undertake serious campaigns to win real victories that demonstrate the value of such organizations to ordinary people's lives, whether that's taking a visible lead in pushing for a Bernie Sanders presidency, or investing months into an intensive strike support effort, or organizing against racist policing or gentrification in their cities.

Socialist organizations tend to grow stale and strange when they are isolated from the working class and disengaged from direct class struggle. But when they aren't, they have the potential to carve out a new type of space in society—a space where working people can learn to work together and lead, expand their ideas and deepen their commitment, and develop a strong socialist identity that will carry them through decades of struggle.

A Long-Distance Race

In addition to every other function we've covered, a socialist organization can provide moral support for people who have been radicalized and have devoted themselves to active struggle. If they don't have that support, they will find the task too immense and hostile to bear. A socialist organization must be much more than a friendship clique or a support group—but we shouldn't discount the importance of friendship and support in sustaining the intense activity required to transform politics. We are, as founder of DSA Michael Harrington put it, running a long-distance race, and we can't afford to lose committed people along the way.

In order to achieve socialism, we must train and sustain a whole new generation of socialist activists, and no other type of formation can do this besides a socialist organization. The ideal form of socialist organization is an independent socialist party, which behaves not merely as an electoral vehicle but as a general hub of socialist organizing. A party with a coherent socialist ideology can connect the dots between all the different arenas of struggle, from labor to the ballot box, from crucial fights against oppression to the urgent efforts to forestall climate disaster. It can be a political home for all who dream of a world beyond capitalism and are willing to fight for it.

Sanders, for all that he has done to revive socialism in America, hasn't prioritized building real grassroots organizations to take what he calls the "political revolution" beyond the electoral sphere. His own organization, Our Revolution, has become a player in the progressive landscape but remains confined to electoral politics—and isn't an explicitly socialist organization. We need a political vehicle for people who want to do more than campaign during election season, and a socialist organization is uniquely suited to this task.

We owe Sanders a great deal for spurring socialism's growth, but we're building something bigger than Bernie. He's busy raising expectations, picking fights with billionaires, and resurrecting class politics. If we want to take advantage of the opening he creates with his own interventions and construct an organization that can outlast him, and that can ensure that socialism is more than just a passing trend, then we'll have to do it ourselves.

5

Engines of Solidarity

In political discussions sparked by the new socialist movement in America, one hears frequent mention of European countries like Sweden, Norway, Denmark, France, and the Netherlands. These countries have successfully pried many essential goods and services out of capitalists' hands, or at least loosened their grip. They have strong welfare states, with key provisions like health care and education either partially or fully funded.

Some commentators speculate that the reason these countries have more guaranteed social rights has to do with characteristics inherent to their cultures (and absent from ours). But that's not true. In all of these countries socialists, unionists, and class-conscious workers played a major role in winning the expansion of the welfare state and the reduction of economic inequality. As a result, while subject to increasing austerity in recent years, millions of people in these countries still live in elevated conditions today because of the workers' struggles of decades past. If we build a strong socialist current and labor movement, we can have nice things, too.

In popular discussion, these countries are often called "socialist" or "democratic socialist." But this isn't quite right either. They are actually social democracies: capitalist societies with a strong social safety net and high progressive taxation. (It's truly confusing and unfortunate that "social democracy" and "democratic socialism" are almost the same phrase but flipped around; even more confounding is the fact that revolutionary socialists once used the phrase "social democracy" to refer to what we now call a socialist society.)

European social democracies have successfully instituted checks on domestic capitalist power. Those victories should be celebrated and defended. They allow those countries' citizens degrees of freedom and security that people elsewhere lack. By showing how much better life can be through decommodification and the universal provision of public goods, social democracies hint at the promise of a socialist society.

The main problem with social democratic countries is that the gains they've made are tenuous. That's because the capitalist class still remains in the driver's seat in those countries. Capitalists aren't happy when they can't make endless amounts of money off expensive housing or health care. Nor are they pleased when they have to pay high taxes for social welfare benefits, or when workers are less afraid to tell them to "take this job and shove it" because society has ensured their basic needs are met. But in social democracies, capitalists are still able to make profits and maintain power in society. In fact, historically, they have mostly acceded to social democratic demands during economic boom times. When economic conditions change, as they did in the 1970s, capitalists inevitably begin fighting hard to claw back all the gains made by workers.

This is what has happened in social democratic states in Europe over the last several decades. Take Sweden, often held up as the best example of social democracy. A strong labor

movement and left electoral coalition made up of social democrats, socialists and communists, and unions dominated the
country's politics for decades, winning democratic election
after election, constructing the strongest social welfare state
in world history, and making solidaristic values synonymous
with Swedishness. That coalition even showed a willingness
to go further than a robust welfare state through the Meidner
Plan, a proposal by Swedish economist Rudolf Meidner that,
among other things, would have led to workers taking control
of the country's major industries through a collectively owned
wage-earner fund that gradually bought up shares in large
companies and distributed the surplus to the benefit of
workers.

But Swedish capital fought back against the plan, eventually
watering it down so much that it was practically defeated.
And as capital regained its footing beginning in the 1980s
and into the '90s, Sweden's Social Democratic Party moved
rightward, and some of their political opponents began to
gain traction in attacking the welfare state as well as the
rising immigrant population in the country. Sweden still has
the strongest welfare state in the world today, but in 2013,
the country also boasted the world's fastest-growing economic
inequality over the previous decade.

Socialists have much to learn from how such a strong social
democratic consensus was built in Sweden over the twentieth
century, but we also must draw lessons from Swedish retrench-
ment. A strong social democracy can't be the horizon of our
ambitions. If our society is successful in reversing the worst
trends of neoliberalism, we will at some point need to face the
fact that social democracy is an unstable system built on shaky
compromises with capitalists that must eventually be transcended to prevent those capitalists from wiping away our gains.

Other attempts to build socialism have failed more spectac-ularly, and are now wielded as a cudgel against twenty-first-century socialists. Some of those attempts, like in the Soviet Union and China, were plagued by problems both from without and within: economic underdevelopment and instability, a turn toward authoritarianism and violence in the face of economic and political crises, corruption and incompetence, and exter-nal sabotage—problems that bear down on capitalist nations, too. There are no easy solutions to these problems, though socialists today are committed to attempting in earnest to avoid the mistakes of the past. The histories of those countries are messy; parsing what they did wrong (a lot) and what they did right (more than a few things) is a task far beyond the scope of this book.

Democratic socialists have always been strong critics of those regimes' degeneration into disastrous, often murderous authoritarianism. Any socialism worthy of the name must center democracy and basic respect for human life. We obvi-ously don't want to emulate authoritarian twentieth-century socialist states like the Soviet Union and China. As much as the Right might insinuate otherwise, socialists today are committed to democracy. In fact, as *Jacobin*'s Shawn Gude has written, "democratic socialism, at its core, is about deep-ening democracy where it exists and introducing democracy where it is absent."

Socialism cannot be reduced to the worst failures of attempts to build socialist states any more than capitalism can be reduced to its most egregious trespasses, from the mass starv-ations of early capitalist India and China to the genocidal plunder of Africa and the Americas. After all, capitalism has brought great misery to many, but it's also been revolutionary, bringing more innovation to the world than its forebears could ever have dreamed. It has hastened the arrival of many useful developments in human civilization and society—even, as Karl Marx himself argued, the eventual ability to transition to socialism. Capitalism's history contains marvels alongside monstrosities.

But capitalists have hoarded the fruits of those developments, as all that innovation has been motivated by private profit and not by a respect for human life and the natural world upon which it depends. For that reason, we are compelled to imagine a world beyond it—egalitarian and democratic, just and free.

Ultimately, our vision for socialism is this: we want to eliminate private ownership of the means of production. We want the principal productive assets of society to be owned in common and run democratically by workers. We want production and work to be allocated democratically according to society's needs, performed not for a boss's enrichment but for public well-being. We want the bounty created by that work to be shared with every member of the society that creates it. And we want everyone to have a meaningful say in what society should look like.

This would be a total political and economic revolution, the end of capitalism and the dawning of socialism. The truth, however, is that all of this is a ways off. It's not as easy as simply saying we want to eliminate capitalism and then making it happen. Capitalism is the law of the land for the time being. What we need right now are strategies to inspire people to organize against it, in their own self-interest and for the common good.

We believe that social democracy is tenuous and unstable, but in the United States today, it would be a vast improvement. Average people understand this intuitively. In the struggle for social democratic reforms, there are enormous opportunities to awaken and cohere working-class movements, which are the vehicle through which we will eventually achieve socialism.

Class-Struggle Social Democracy

If you look at the policy agendas of the socialists who are on the ascent today, such as Bernie Sanders and Alexandria Ocasio-Cortez in the US, many of their proposals could reasonably be called social democratic. Sanders, for example, has proposed eliminating our for-profit health insurance industry and securing free public college for all. These are reforms that have already been implemented in much of the world and that capitalism would easily accommodate and survive. What's so socialist about that?

The answer to this question lies in what Bhaskar Sunkara calls "class-struggle social democracy." This means using the struggle for social democratic reforms to raise class consciousness and activate the working class:

> On the face of it [the then UK Labour Party leader Jeremy] Corbyn and Sanders advocate a set of demands that are essentially social democratic. But they represent something far different from modern social democracy. Whereas social democracy morphed in the postwar period into a tool to suppress class conflict in favor of tripartite arrangements among business, labor, and the state, both of these leaders encourage a renewal of class antagonism and movements from below . . . Class-struggle social democracy, then, is generating working-class strength through electoral campaigns rather than subordinating existing struggles to the goal of getting a few people elected.

In advanced capitalist countries with fraying or borderline-nonexistent welfare states, social democratic demands can be used to help galvanize the types of movements that socialists know are necessary to build in order to push beyond social democracy itself. That doesn't mean that every politician making social democratic demands fits the bill; for example, now that Bernie Sanders has made Medicare for All a popular demand, he has his fair share of imitators. The difference is that class-struggle social democrats don't seek to limit the political horizons or manage the expectations of the working class. Instead they actively elevate expectations, use the rhetoric of class struggle, and foster workers' self-organization at the grassroots level. They don't act as "responsible" political intermediaries for the working class, encouraging average people to avoid anything rash like strikes or other acts of militancy. On the contrary, a class-struggle social democratic strategy is one that sees such militancy as essential for winning short- and long-term gains—and is dedicated to stoking more of it.

No socialist thinks that campaigning for and electing Bernie Sanders or other politicians like him is a silver bullet. Instead, it is an opportunity to give effective political shape to the inchoate anger and resentment that characterizes working-class life, to direct that anger at the people at the top, and to create movements in which working people begin to feel their own power. If Sanders or someone like him became president, the United States would not immediately transform into a socialist society. But Sanders has opened up the intellectual and political space to develop a mass movement of people who are conscious of an alternative to the misery they endure under capitalism, and of their own potential to bring that alternative into being.

Social democratic reforms are insufficient in the grand scheme of things. But such reforms are nothing to sneeze at. They represent massive, life-altering improvements for millions of people who are struggling under our current system. Struggling people are right to want change. And under the right conditions, history has shown that they are willing to fight for it—especially if they think they can win it. That fight is at the center of socialist strategy. It is in the struggle for reforms under capitalism that the infrastructure of a workers' movement is built up, and people learn the lessons and acquire the skills necessary to go toe-to-toe with the capitalist class.

Additionally, the more successful we are at winning ambitious reforms, the more open the capitalist class becomes in its attempts to undermine workers' gains (as opposed to the present, where they skate by on the image of themselves as benevolent elites). That's a fight worth having, especially if we're strong enough after decades of struggle to potentially emerge victorious. As Sunkara writes, "The route to a more radical socialism will come from the crisis of social democracy our very success initiates. Class-struggle social democracy, then, isn't a foe of democratic socialism—the road to the latter runs through the former."

Reform and Revolution

The idea that socialists should make use of the struggle for reforms to build our forces is hardly new. "Can [socialists] be against reforms?" asked Rosa Luxemburg, a revolutionary socialist who rose to prominence through the German Social Democratic Party in the late nineteenth century. "Can we contrapose the social revolution, the transformation of the existing order, our final goal, to social reforms? Certainly not."

Luxemburg distinguished her view from that of reformists, who naively believed in the "gradual realization of socialism through social reforms" alone. These reformists elicited the bulk of her criticism. But she insisted that reforms still played a major role in inspiring, educating, organizing, and empowering mass numbers of people:

> The daily struggle for reforms, for the amelioration of the condition of the workers within the framework of the existing social order, and for democratic institutions, offers to [socialists] the only means of engaging in the proletarian class war and working in the direction of the final goal—the conquest of political power and the suppression of wage labour. Between social reforms and revolution there exists for [socialists] an indissoluble tie. The struggle for reforms is its means; the social revolution, its aim.

Reforms are by their nature incomplete, but struggles for reforms have always been central to the strategy of advancing the socialist movement. Reforms are only the beginning, but marginalized socialists cannot build a mass movement by demanding immediate revolution and rejecting all reforms as inadequate. That approach is not a recipe for mass politics.

The immediate task of socialists is to pick fights with elites, and to stand with workers wherever they find themselves already engaged in struggle. Crucial to this strategy is the identification of the right demands for reform. The reforms that we choose to throw our weight behind must be strategically selected in light of social and political conditions. They must be chosen by assessing the needs and desires of the working class, and balancing this against an assessment of the strengths and weaknesses of the capitalist system.

To create optimal conditions for socialist agitation in the future, reform struggles should be designed to draw out class conflict: victories for the working class should be won by taking something away from the capitalist class, prompting them to fight back. This clarifies the lines between those capitalists and workers. Ideally, reforms advocated by socialists also put socialist values into motion, such as the value of decommodification, or taking a needed good or service out of private hands and placing it in public hands. The best reforms, once won, will also erode the power the capitalist class has over workers, making it easier for the working class to organize, fight, and win more in the future.

There are some reforms that—if fought for strategically and won on the right terms—position us better to square off with capitalists down the line, and not get obliterated in the process. The Austrian socialist André Gorz called this kind of reform a "structural reform." A structural reform cannot simply be an improvement in the immediate state of affairs; it has to involve a transfer of significant power from capital to labor, "a victory of democracy over the dictatorship of profit," and point to a world beyond capitalism.

An example of this kind of demand for American socialists living in the nineteenth century was the fight for the eight-hour workday. Obviously, that demand fell significantly short of socialists' ultimate goal, which was the abolition of wage labor. But the demand spoke to workers' real needs and forced them to ask questions about the system they were living and working under. The International Workingmen's Association, of which Karl Marx himself was a leader, made this a central demand, even though they were also very clear that they ultimately desired the abolition of the wage system. Winning the eight-hour day, and eventually overtime pay, didn't overturn capitalism. But it did transfer power from bosses to workers—ushering in a new reality in which workers could lay claim to their own time—as well as awaken many workers' passion and consciousness in the process.

What would such a structural reform look like in the United States today? The best example is Medicare for All. Millions of people across the country are drowning in medical debt, rationing costly medicine, forgoing necessary care because it's too expensive. Despite the gains of Obamacare, millions of Americans still remain uninsured. A Medicare for All system would fix all that.

It's not the end goal for socialists: we want to decommodify all health care, not just health insurance, and we would eventually like to decommodify spheres well beyond health care itself. But eliminating insurance companies and instituting a single-payer health care program is a reform that could potentially inspire the working class to fight for its own interests against capitalists, and in the process discover the true nature of class conflict. It could also transfer power to the working class. Right now, millions of people stay in jobs where they are mistreated and underpaid because they need the employer-provided health care benefits, while unions forgo fights to demand higher wages or other forms of compensation because they're forced to focus on securing those benefits. With health insurance provided automatically and universally, workers could be freer to tell their bosses to shove it, while unions could negotiate over more ambitious demands.

A single reform like Medicare for All won't end capitalism, not even in the realm of health care. Some sectors of the capitalist class may even find that Medicare for All is in their own short-term profit interest—though the cleverest among them will interpret it as an attack on their class's dominance.

Still, fighting for Medicare for All emboldens ordinary people to imagine new political possibilities, to make new claims on the future. And it trains them for bigger battles to come. If working people saw success in a fight to end for-profit health insurance, what other for-profit institutions might they decide need to be decommodified and reorganized for the public good?

Medicare for All is only one example. American workers' wages remain low while profits skyrocket, and our welfare state has been eviscerated by neoliberal austerity policy. Taxing the rich, raising wages, and building up the welfare state with programs like free higher education, universal childcare, and a job guarantee tethered to a Green New Deal are all mean-ingful projects with obvious benefits to working people. These struggles can put working people into motion against the capitalist class and give socialists the opportunity to agitate against the capitalist elites who oppose them, building class consciousness and strengthening our movement for more ambitious fights. The nature of the *reforms* may be social democratic, but the nature of the *fight* can be socialist, so long as it is undertaken in the spirit of building our forces for future battles down the line.

The current crop of class-struggle social democrats is inject-ing these ideas into the mainstream. That's a good reason for socialists to be enthusiastic about their brand of politics. But it's not just the reforms these politicians propose that enthuse socialists; it's also the way they frame what it will take to win them, and to eventually win the society we deserve.

The most striking feature about the Sanders campaign is how it emphasizes the power that ordinary working people hold, as long as they are conscious and courageous enough to wield it. For example, in a video his campaign released in

2019, Sanders can be heard speaking over footage of strikes and protests, beginning with the Memphis sanitation workers' 1968 strike (the same strikers to whom Martin Luther King Jr. spoke as his last act, the night before he was murdered). Sanders says,

> Nothing will change unless we have the guts to take on Wall Street, the insurance industry, the pharmaceutical industry, the military-industrial complex, and the fossil fuel industry. It is not good enough to talk about great ideas. They're important, but nothing happens unless people look around them and say, "You know what, this status quo is not working. It's not just, it's not right, it's not fair."
>
> I want you to think about this, think about real change in America. The labor movement was created when millions of workers stood up and said, "You know what, you're going to treat us with dignity and respect. We're gonna have collective bargaining." It wasn't somebody at the top who made that decision.

The core message was that change cannot be left up to political elites who claim to have people's best interests at heart. Change must come from the vast majority, united in struggle, fighting for itself.

Bernie has gone out of his way to discuss his admiration for Franklin Delano Roosevelt, so it's understandable when some suggest he's just a left-wing liberal erroneously referring to himself as a democratic socialist. But while Roosevelt inveighed eloquently against inequality as he sought to implement major pro-worker reforms, he did not call for mass political activity from below. That activity was already all around him, to the point where he and political and business leaders like him were truly worried about a revolution popping off in the country. FDR wanted to figure out how to tamp down those conflicts.

By contrast, it was Eugene Debs who spoke of the power of working people to change the world despite the considerable political advantages of elites. You could say that Sanders has a Debs-style approach to advocating for FDR-style policies, with the intention of positioning the working class to demand much more in the future.

To move beyond social democracy and into a true socialist society, we will need a serious, coherent, mass working-class socialist movement that fights for the economic and political rights of the majority, and knows they can only be secured by confronting the wealthy few. Again, we're currently a ways off from realizing that kind of movement. The task now is to lay the groundwork for its emergence. By returning class struggle to the US political mainstream for the first time in decades, that's precisely what Sanders and others are attempting to do.

In this context, class-struggle social democratic politics perform an important task—probably the most important task for socialists at the beginning of our movement's twenty-first-century resurgence. We must convince ordinary people of the fundamental principles at the heart of the Marxist theory of social change: that their power is greater than they know, and that the fate of the world rests in their hands.

Engines of Solidarity

Class-struggle politicians, like all politicians, have to run on a platform. What should that platform look like? As with everything a class-struggle politician does, the platform must set working people's sights higher than before, and unite them together against a common capitalist adversary.

There is one kind of demand that deserves special attention, because it holds special promise. That is the demand for universal social programs.

Universal social programs apply to everyone, without eligibility requirements. By providing a public service to all people, no questions asked, they reject the patchwork approach of a social welfare system with highly stringent requirements on who gets what benefits. The social spending they require is offset by universal progressive taxes, meaning everyone pays what they can to sustain a system that provides for all; from each according to their ability, to each according to their need. The rich will bear most of the cost burden—but the rich will get to use these programs, too. Even as they soak the rich to serve the poor, universal social programs still enshrine certain benefits as rights to be enjoyed by all. This helps build a broad constituency that can be mobilized in defense of these programs, thus thwarting the attempts of reactionary and opportunistic politicians who want to starve or eliminate them.

Democrats don't usually go for universal social programs these days. Instead they prefer means-tested programs, which are restricted to people who "really need" assistance, as opposed to those who can presumably help themselves. You can see this logic at play in the rhetoric of Sanders's Democratic primary opponent Pete Buttigieg, who objected to tuition-free public college on the basis that it supposedly constitutes a handout to wealthy people who can afford college on their own. Of course, this is a smokescreen: the wealthy will pay for tuition-free public college in higher taxes, which negates the idea of a handout. And, besides, wealthy people send their children to private colleges anyway, which will end up costing them even more. What Buttigieg really opposed, on principle, is the universal design of tuition-free public college. Like all centrist Democrats, he preferred a less comprehensive approach to social programs instead, and found a clever way of communicating his preference that made it appear that he had the best interests of the working class at heart, when the opposite was true.

Why do Democrats like means testing so much? Because they cost less public money than universal social programs, of course. Means testing allows Democrats to limit taxes on their ruling-class donor base while still superficially appeasing their working-class voter base. They also like means-tested programs because such programs simply aren't as durable for the long term. Means testing is therefore a perfect complement to Democrats' cross-class balancing act.

On a deeper level, a robust social welfare state means an empowered working class. If workers have a strong social safety net to fall back on, the threat of ending up in complete penury for leaving a job is no longer as great, which means workers are less subordinate and less easily exploitable. They can bargain harder for higher wages and better benefits, and their gains eat into employer's profits. Capitalists don't like that, so it's in their interests to resist the creation of a strong social welfare state. Democrats hear those concerns, and settle on means testing as a compromise. That way they can claim to their working-class supporters that they're taking social problems seriously without biting the hand that feeds them.

The party doesn't say any of this out loud, though. Generally, Democrats say that limiting the provision of social services to targeted groups is the best way to use our scarce resources to provide for people who are actually in need. They never acknowledge the possibility that our resources aren't actually scarce, but purposefully *starved* for the many so they can be hoarded by the few—and that we could pry some of those resources out of the hands of the rich if we picked a fight with them. Whether it's because Democrats are daunted by the prospect of biting the hand that feeds them or because they genuinely think the rich deserve what they've got isn't always clear. Either way, means testing is an expression of establishment Democrats' timid middle-ground politics.

A major problem with means-tested social programs is they are a nightmare both for the administrator and the participant. They are designed to differentiate, cherry-pick, and exclude, which means they're guarded by miles of red tape. The process of enrolling is often elaborate, the criteria convoluted and stringent, and the thresholds arbitrary, meaning that people swiftly move in and out of eligibility without dramatic changes in their actual level of need. People frequently get dropped from programs without warning, forcing them to drastically change course in their personal lives. And the benefits are rarely complete—the majority of federal student aid recipients take out loans, just as many welfare recipients turn to payday lenders and whatever other means they can scrape together to pay the bills.

This is actually part of means testing's appeal for centrist politicians who have made promises to both the rich and the rest. The more difficult it is for people to prove themselves deserving of aid, the less likely they will be to successfully secure that aid. This means fewer program enrollees, which saves money, and that allows politicians to get away with slashing taxes for the rich and balancing budgets, all while continuing to promise the working class that they have its best interests at heart. It's a win-win-win for centrist politicians, and a victory for the wealthy. But the working class—thwarted, puzzled, intimidated, maybe even unaware of the program's existence in the first place—loses.

Means-tested programs are held up as evidence that a politician or party is taking a particular social problem, like staggering tuition and student debt, under serious consideration. But for far too many people, these programs don't actually provide the relief they promise on the scale they claim. That failure is actually built into the model.

In addition to being administratively nightmarish, means-tested programs are politically flimsy. Or in other words, targeted programs make easy targets. From health care to housing to education, those who are struggling but don't qualify for aid are quick to become resentful of those who do, and this resentment is easy for politicians to exploit as they seek to erode and eliminate social benefits. When you set strict parameters around who qualifies for aid, you invite conservative elements to aggressively renegotiate the parameters—a battle pitched in their favor. Any program designed for the "deserving poor" can be undermined by evoking the specter of the "undeserving poor."

For example, Medicaid is specifically for low-income people. It is often portrayed as a charitable gift that society's more privileged members furnish for its most vulnerable. Naturally, conservatives leap at the opportunity to renegotiate the terms of the gift. "For any politician who loathes government interventions in the economy, and whose real goal is to head off socialized medicine, the expansion of Medicaid represents a serious threat. Here is an embryonic single-payer system that is growing fast and could be further expanded pretty easily," wrote the *New Yorker*'s John Cassidy in 2017. "That means it has to be crippled now, before it gets more firmly established."

This is why Republicans vehemently opposed the expansion of Medicaid under President Barack Obama, and why so many Republicans and some Democrats support adding work requirements as a condition of Medicaid eligibility.

The stated purpose of work requirements for Medicaid is to induce lazy people to get jobs. (Never mind that the vast majority of Medicaid recipients already have jobs, while many more wish they had jobs but can't find them.) But the real purpose is to frustrate the enrollment process and thin the rolls to make room in state budgets. Meanwhile, the rhetoric politicians use to justify their assault on means-tested social programs is dripping with resentment and blame. "We owe our fellow citizens more than just giving them a Medicaid card. We owe a card with care, and more importantly a card with hope," Trump's administrator of the Centers for Medicare and Medicaid Services said in 2017 to justify expanding work requirements. "Hope that they can break the chains of generational poverty and no longer need public assistance."

Statements like this are designed to stigmatize recipients, sow distrust, and fan the flames of prejudice. In particular, it's common for opportunistic politicians to use racist and xenophobic dog whistles in an attempt to convince people that austerity is actually desirable, because it will stop *those people* from sponging off the system. Political fights over the parameters of these programs are therefore a recipe for heightened hostility and eroded solidarity in the broader culture. Debates over means-tested programs often further entrench preexisting bigotry.

Partners in Prosperity

So, to recap, under means testing, people who might qualify for aid are easily discouraged by the headache-inducing bureaucracy they must navigate to secure it. Those who don't are easily convinced that recipients are undeserving. All of this makes means-tested programs generally unpopular and politically fragile. As DSA member and *Jacobin* contributor Robbie Nelson has written,

> Meager, means-tested social programs have become liberals' bread and butter over the past thirty years. Unfortunately, these programs don't win broad-based support. A large body of research—and a cursory look at opinion polling—indicates that universal programs like Medicare and Social Security are the most consistently popular, and the most difficult to erode legislatively.

Universal social programs operate by a totally different logic than means-tested programs. They materialize when a society decides that it wants a certain opportunity to be enshrined as a social right. And they enhance solidarity, not bigotry.

We have public K-12 schools in this country because we decided that adolescent education was a basic right that should be enjoyed by all, because society is better that way. We have a universal postal system because we decided that we should all be able to send and receive mail—even those who live in remote, rural areas—and we agreed to pay taxes based on income to make it possible. We have Social Security and Medicare because we concluded that all people—us, our friends, our enemies—ought to be able to live out their twilight years with dignity. We do not have a public health insurance system yet, but increasingly the American public is realizing that health care ought to be one of those things that everyone pays for and everyone gets, because the alternative is barbaric and dehumanizing.

If means-tested programs are chaotic and politically delicate, universal programs are more elegant and politically sturdy. If means testing is an engine of division, then universality is, as Nelson has written, "an engine of solidarity."

At their best, universal social programs engender in people a sense of collective investment and common cause. Everybody chips in what they can, and everybody enjoys the fruits of their contributions. The programs are accessible, legible, and visible to all. Universal social programs feel not like begrudging charity but like a mutual endeavor, for which all bear responsibility and from which all benefit. Society is elevated by mass participation and collaboration.

With the exception of the very wealthy, most of whom will always resent having to pay high taxes for things they can personally afford on their own, people who live in societies with guaranteed social rights can come to view each other not as obstacles to individual success, but as partners in prosperity. Where a bare-bones, means-tested model breeds alienation and competition, a robust universal-welfare model fosters trust and cooperation. These qualities are necessary to develop a foundation from which to launch other ambitious social projects and to progress as a society.

Universal social programs are not completely invulnerable to attack—consider the encroachment of charter schools as part of the broader attempt to dismantle and privatize the existing public school system in the United States. But they do create mass constituencies willing to defend them—constituencies that might not otherwise exist—such as when teachers, parents, and students recently mobilized to defend public education in a wave of militant teachers' strikes. When social goods are enshrined as rights, they are not so easily taken away.

Another example is Social Security. Despite the desperate desire of many Republicans and more than a few Democrats (including both of our previous two Democratic presidents) to privatize and diminish Social Security, they can't—the program is far too popular. It's so popular because it covers *all* seniors, not just seniors who are poor. The constituency for the program is universal; everyone thus has a stake in defending it. If the program only covered cash-strapped seniors, Republican and Democratic politicians who wanted to abolish Social Security could demonize and stigmatize those recipients as undeserving, lazy old people who should've planned better for retirement but are instead sponging off the American taxpayer, the way many members of both parties did during the debates over welfare reform under Bill Clinton in the 1990s. The results would be devastating for low-income American seniors.

Socialists know that the best way to build programs that can withstand inevitable attempts at unraveling is to make them universal, so that they can become popular, beloved, and woven into the fabric of our culture. Including these programs—like Medicare for All, a job guarantee, tuition-free public college, and paid parental leave—in class-struggle politicians' platforms is key for two reasons. One, because in order to win them, we have to popularize them. We have to get buy-in from the working class, which is currently beaten down after decades of their society telling them that decent provisions like health care, employment, and time off work to spend with their newborn children are privileges, not rights.

Two, because in the process of raising the working class's expectations about what it deserves from society (and specifically from society's ruling class, which will pay more in taxes to fund these programs *and* lose out on the chance to profit from their commodification), universal social programs have the ability to unite people who are otherwise divided by culture, geography, race, national origin, gender, sexuality, religion, and other forms of difference.

Socialists do not want to elide these differences altogether, nor are we opposed to reforms that provide remedies for specific demographics with unique concerns. Our society is marred by oppression, and racial, gender, and other forms of difference play a critical role in shaping the material and emotional realities of our lives. But one of the primary functions of oppression is to divide the working class, to prevent it from locating common cause and uniting in common struggle. Universal social programs speak to material needs that cut across lines of difference—the need for health care, for example—and give a divided working class an opportunity to fight in unison, to demonstrate solidarity.

Democrats claim to stand against oppression, but the means-tested programs they champion divide people. Demands for universal social programs, on the other hand, give the working class a real opportunity to come together. They do this not by erasing conflict, but by imagining a new "us versus them": all members of the working class united against the tiny number of capitalists that conspire to keep them down.

At their very best, universal social programs can be an anchor in a broader political and social project to bring people together across all kinds of difference and see one another as partners in prosperity, whose interests and destinies are intertwined. Martin Luther King Jr. wrote that we live "in an inescapable network of mutuality, tied in a single garment of destiny. Whatever affects one directly, affects all indirectly." Capitalism, especially in its neoliberal form in recent decades, has dismantled any sense that we all belong to such a common project with the rest of humanity. Universal social programs offer one key way to rebuild that common project.

The Bully Pulpit

Let's say we've accepted the strategic need to pursue structural reforms, we want to do it in a way that builds class struggle, and we've got an ambitious, unifying platform that expands the horizon of political possibility while still speaking to people's real material needs—one that places special emphasis on universal social programs. What do we do next?

When we're a political minority in a representative body, it's not possible to govern directly, simply muscling through legislation of our own devising. Our means have to be more indirect. Medicare for All is far from a done deal—the private insurance and pharmaceutical lobbies are planning to fight it with everything they've got, in concert with their allies in both parties. They've already started doing so, with assistance from their centrist friends in the Democratic Party. But Medicare for All has become a mainstream idea thanks in large part to Sanders's popular agitation. When socialist elected officials have few friends in the halls of power, they have to use their platforms as a bully pulpit.

Alexandria Ocasio-Cortez is a natural agitator of exactly this kind. Together with Rashida Tlaib and Ilhan Omar, these three make up only a tiny sliver of Congress. But they have outsize power to influence American politics because they are unafraid to pick fights and make bold claims and demands that appeal to ordinary people's beliefs about justice and fairness. In the process, they have expanded the horizons of political possibility in the United States. Even as a tiny minority, they can constitute a real threat to established power, aerating the soil in which socialist ideas can take root and flourish.

One of the first things Alexandria Ocasio-Cortez did as a new member of Congress was introduce legislation for a Green New Deal. The story of the Green New Deal so far is a case study in how a political minority can use the office as a bully pulpit.

Right out of the gate, Ocasio-Cortez's Green New Deal proposal was a declaration of class war, in a way that acts as an engine of solidarity. Its objective is to meet all of the power demand in the United States with renewable and zero-emissions energy. This will require a massive coordinated effort to develop, upgrade, and replace our infrastructure, from building new energy-efficient power grids to outfitting existing buildings for maximum sustainability. It means investing in zero-emissions vehicle manufacturing, public transit, and high-speed rail. And it will require overhauling our agriculture and food systems, publicly funding research and development in ecology and energy, and restoring and protecting fragile ecosystems. "This is going to be the New Deal, the Great Society, the moon shot, the civil rights movement of our generation," Ocasio-Cortez said about the proposal.

The Green New Deal breaks from the dominant approach of fighting climate change and environmental destruction in the last few decades: individualistic, consumer-focused, guilt-laced appeals to save a poor polar bear drifting out to see on an ice floe by using eco-friendly light bulbs. Those light bulbs have a place in an environmentally sustainable society, and the polar bear needs our help, too. But lecturing average Americans about their individual consumption is a political dead end for saving the planet—particularly when the American working class has been under the vicious and continued assault of austerity and union-busting in their communities and their jobs over the last four decades.

Adbusters, the anticonsumerist magazine that made the initial call for Occupy Wall Street, once released a video about consumption that depicted average Americans as literal pigs. This kind of framing, dripping with contempt for ordinary people who didn't choose to live in a society organized around environmentally destructive consumption, has no political future. If we see the working class as the agent of social change on the environment and every other burning political issue, we can't accuse working-class people of being greedy piggies gobbling up the planet's resources—especially since average US workers don't live opulently, unlike US ultra-wealthy elites, whose consumption habits are not only garish but many orders of magnitude more environmentally destructive than the average American's. Anti–climate change legislation must go after those elites, not workers, and must focus on the environmental devastation wrought by the major industries they head

The Green New Deal proposal understands this. It does not demonize average people, nor workers who work in the extractive industries like coal and oil that are killing the planet. Instead, it proposes a "just transition" for those workers that wouldn't leave them high and dry in the transition away from fossil fuels, but instead would train them and put them to work in new green energy jobs. This is the only way we can win such workers to our side rather than driving them into the open arms of the Right.

The bill calls for the creation of millions of high-wage union jobs to make the necessary transitions. This proposal would likely amount to a de facto job guarantee, as it could bring the nation up to full employment, functionally guaranteeing a job to anyone who wants one. But the bill goes one step further and makes the job guarantee explicit. It sets as a goal "guaranteeing a job with a family-sustaining wage, adequate family and medical leave, paid vacations, and retirement security to all people of the United States."

A job guarantee was an explicit demand of the civil rights movement. The full title of the 1963 March on Washington, organized in large part by socialists including A. Philip Randolph, Bayard Rustin, and Martin Luther King Jr. himself, was the March on Washington for Jobs and Freedom. In *A Freedom Budget for All Americans*, a 1966 pamphlet authored by the three men, a job guarantee was a central demand. The first of its seven demands was "to provide full employment for all who are willing and able to work."

In the 1970s the New American Movement, which later merged with the Democratic Socialist Organizing Committee to form DSA, printed a poster that explained socialists' thinking on a job guarantee beautifully:

> If you're unemployed, it's not because there isn't any work. Just look around: a housing shortage, crime, pollution; we need better schools and parks. Whatever our needs, they all require work. And as long as we have unsatisfied needs, there is work to be done. So ask yourself, what kind of world has work but no jobs? It's a world where work is not related to satisfying our needs, a world where work is only related to satisfying the profit needs of business.

Despite a long legacy, the demand has been off the table for decades. Now it's back, as key piece of a plan to fight climate change.

Education and training will be required to prepare the workforce for this heroic effort. The bill calls for the provision of those, too, free of cost to all. And how can we ensure that our people are healthy and stable enough to participate fully in this monumental collective undertaking? The bill affirms the right of all people to high-quality health care and safe, affordable housing. For good measure, it identifies economic security for everyone as a necessary component of a Green New Deal.

A bold plan pitched to benefit rather than dispossess the working class—thus inviting mass participation from ordinary people who might otherwise feel alienated by the environmentalist movement—can potentially pull us back from the brink of climate annihilation. But it will hurt the profit margins of some very powerful people in the process. The Green New Deal says, *Who cares?* Our collective future is more important than their private bank accounts.

Ocasio-Cortez's Green New Deal resolution aims to take on the fossil fuel industry, planning to reduce greenhouse gas emissions by 40 percent to 60 percent by 2030 and achieve net-zero global emissions by 2050. This is required to keep the planet below 1.5 degrees Celsius above pre-industrial levels and thereby reduce the severity of major storms, wildfires, sea level rise, and all the chaos those climate-related events entail. It's feasible, so long as we can muster the political will to place the well-being of the global majority over the financial mandates of a handful of capitalists who will happily burn the planet to a crisp if we let them maintain the status quo.

Ocasio-Cortez's Green New Deal resolution is an opening gambit. The project it lays out can't be accomplished by a single piece of legislation, and though it must be undertaken immediately, it must also be measured in decades. The resolution calls the Green New Deal a "national mobilization"—like when a nation mobilizes for war. But in this case, as with the original US New Deal, lives will be saved and improved rather than destroyed. And the war will be waged not against another nation, but against a common threat to the people of all nations.

Green Dream

On the one hand, the plans' prospects appear bleak. Democrats won a narrow majority in the House in 2018, but Republicans still control the Senate—and Republicans are backed by oil money. Not only that, but mainstream Democrats are notoriously non-reactive to the threat of climate change—or worse, propose market-friendly measures that don't fundamentally threaten corporate polluters and would effect nowhere near the kind of radical reduction in carbon emissions that we need to avert disaster—and won't automatically be much help in pursuing ambitious solutions like the Green New Deal. Nancy Pelosi responded to Ocasio-Cortez's legislation, and the popular response it elicited, with condescension. "The green dream or whatever they call it," she quipped, "nobody knows what it is, but they're for it, right?"

So despite the ticking clock on climate disaster, the Green New Deal's passage is not imminent. But the idea is on the table, and pressure to do something ambitious to stop climate change is mounting. And that's because Ocasio-Cortez had the audacity to propose a piece of legislation that was necessary; that had a preexisting popular constituency among the millions of Americans deeply worried about climate change; and that capitalist allies in the Democratic and Republican Parties were never going to propose themselves, regardless of how dire the climate situation got.

Ocasio-Cortez's popularization of the Green New Deal is a perfect example of how democratic socialists, even as extreme political minorities, can use their platforms as bully pulpits—agitating for working-class demands, picking fights with capitalist elites, evoking universality and solidarity, and dramatically raising expectations. Even when we're small in number, we can still be tribunes for socialism. We can provide new vocabulary, widen the scope of the possible, and ignite new passions and understandings among millions of people.

If anyone but the ultra-wealthy on this planet is to avoid the apocalyptic effects of climate change, we will need the Green New Deal. A massive restructuring, retooling, and reprioritizing of every aspect of our society is required to save the planet. And we'll have to approach the Green New Deal as we approach every other fight: by advancing policies that not only make people's lives better but that bind us all together in a common project for our mutual salvation.

Neoliberal policies foster isolation, competition, and prejudice. We must build a new consensus, and suffuse political life with the idea that we're all in this together. It's the truth, and it also happens to be our only way forward.

6

Rank-and-File Revolution

As individuals, workers are less powerful than the people they work for. Capitalists have more money and more political power, and they really don't want to share. But capitalism does have an Achilles' heel: owners also rely on the continuous labor of workers to generate profit.

Workers are the linchpin of the entire economic system. As the American socialist leader Eugene V. Debs put it in 1894, "But for labor no keel would cleave the waves nor locomotives speed along their iron tracks. The warehouses would stand empty, factories would be silent, ships and docks would rot, cities would tumble down, and universal ruin would prevail." While neither of us know exactly what a "keel" is, Debs is right to argue that if workers became conscious of this power they wielded, they could act in concert to grind the system to a halt—and replace it with a new one.

This isn't just a hypothetical, theoretical claim cooked up by some socialist academics with a fantastical imagination. In 1934, truck drivers who were members of Teamsters Local 574 in Minneapolis walked off the job, one of three general strikes that kicked off separately that year. The city of

Minneapolis was paralyzed. The truckers' strike itself had a huge impact, affecting most businesses in the city. But it exploded when other workers joined the strike in solidarity. Jeremy Brecher writes,

> Support for the strike among other Minneapolis workers was passionate. Thirty-five thousand building trades workers walked out in sympathy, as did all the taxi drivers in the city. The Farm Holiday Association, a militant farmers' organization, made substantial contributions of food, and other unions contributed to the strike fund. Hundreds of non-Teamster workers showed up at strike headquarters daily, saying, "Use us, this is our strike."

You don't have to look that far back in history to see this kind of power. In the recent teachers' strike wave, in cities like Chicago and Los Angeles and states like West Virginia and Arizona, few people could go about their daily lives without either needing to adjust their routines to the temporary reality of shuttered schools or encountering the ubiquitous presence of striking teachers, whether picketing at local schools or marching en masse in city downtowns or on state capitols by the thousands.

In such moments of upsurge, workers have not just stopped the production process; they've created a miniature version of a world in which the many are in charge, not the few. During the Seattle General Strike of 1919, for example, Brecher writes that

> workers improvised large-scale operations from scratch. For instance, the milk wagon drivers initially proposed to the employers that certain dairies remain open, but when the

employers refused to open any dairies except in downtown Seattle, and attempted to take direction of the plan, the drivers decided to organize their own distribution system instead. They set up thirty-five neighborhood milk stations, purchased milk from small dairies near the city, and distributed it throughout Seattle. Even more impressive was the commissary department, which served 30,000 meals a day to the strikers and community. The cooks, waiters, and other provision trade workers purchased the food, located restaurant kitchens, and arranged to transport the cooked food to twenty-one eating places in halls throughout the city. This huge operation was running smoothly by the second day of the strike.

For a political revolution to have any chance of succeeding, the working class must come to see itself as a class, with interests that are opposite those of the capitalists, as they have in these moments. Everything socialists do is aimed toward fostering that evolution of the working class into a self-conscious and self-confident political force that fights on its own behalf. The organized working class has to be the anchor of a broader movement to bring about socialism, not only because workers form a social majority, but also because they are the ones who have the means and the motive to hit capitalists where it hurts—or to create a political crisis through a public employee strike. Socialism can play a crucial role in providing that coherence, and can help campaigns for justice of all kinds root themselves in the working class. That class orientation should anchor fights against racism, sexism, homophobia, xenophobia, gentrification, war, climate destruction, and much more.

When we refer to the working class, we don't just mean white men in hard hats (though we mean them, too). Class is a complicated and contradictory thing, but broadly speaking a member of the working class is anybody who works for a wage from a boss and is not themselves a boss (or a person with major employee management responsibilities). Some members of the working class make more money or have more autonomy than others, but they share a common location in the production process—they are the ones whose labor produces value that is not returned to them in full, appropriated instead as profit by their employers. And they are the ones who can stop working all together in order to hold profits hostage and demand concessions from the capitalist class. While the working class is diverse in the true sense of the word, it comprises a disproportionate number of women and people of color.

Going forward, the socialist coalition will definitely include people outside the working class, strictly speaking. As the late sociologist Erik Olin Wright argues, socialists in the twenty-first century have to offer an appeal to workers directly, but also calibrate our demands to appeal to an even wider range of people (bodega owners, low-level managers, self-employed artisans, and innumerable others) based on common interests and shared moral values.

But socialists pay special attention to the working class because it is located at the heart of the capitalist system. As Vivek Chibber writes,

> Progressive reform efforts have to find a source of leverage, a source of power that will enable them to overcome the resistance of the capitalist class and its political functionaries. The working class has this power, for a simple reason—capitalists can only make their profits if workers show up to work every day, and if they refuse to play along,

the profits dry up overnight. Actions like strikes don't just have the potential to bring particular capitalists to their knees, they can have an impact far beyond, on layer after layer of other institutions that directly or indirectly depend on them—including the government.

This ability to crash the entire system, just by refusing to work, gives workers a kind of leverage that no other group in society has, except capitalists themselves . . . It is of central importance to organize workers so that they can use that power.

The best way to strategically organize those workers to wield their power is through unions. It's true that unions are often narrowly focused on negotiating with management to secure better wages and conditions for their members. But unions can also give workers the chance to learn what kind of latent power they possess in society, how to build that power by uniting with their coworkers and fighting together, and, in the best-case scenario, realize the urgent need for them to expand their fights beyond their own workplace and industry and toward the entire working class.

Unfortunately, the US labor movement is in severe decline, the weakest it has been in nearly a century. In 2018, only 10.7 percent of workers were members of unions, and a pitiful 6.4 percent in the private sector. Public-sector unions remain a stronghold for labor, but they, too, are under severe attack from the neoliberal establishment, which has successfully eroded those unions' power and reduced the proportion of represented workers across the country.

One reflection of this decline is that workers' use of their ultimate weapon, the strike, is incredibly rare. Though we've seen an important uptick in strikes since the beginning of

2018 (especially among teachers, but in other sectors like health care, hotels, and some industrial strikes like the auto industry, too), those rates are still incredibly low. The labor movement, then, is not in good health. And the consequences are evident all around us. It's not an accident that the rise in economic inequality in the United States almost exactly mirrors the decline in union power since the mid-twentieth century. Unions once redistributed the wealth in the United States to the working class, but as unions have grown weaker, the rich haven't had anyone to stop them from hoarding all that wealth for themselves.

Without a strong, organized working class that can challenge capital at the point of production in the private sector, and challenge government-imposed austerity at all levels in the public sector, we will continue to encounter serious roadblocks to progress. Because the labor movement is so important for both the working class and the broader Left, socialists and everyone else who wants the world to be more fair and just have an active interest in rebuilding the labor movement.

The Sanders campaign has not only put class politics back on the map at an electoral level, but also helped stir organizing and militancy at workplaces throughout the country. The whole point of raising expectations about what working people should expect in their lives—a living wage, affordable housing, free health care, dignity on the job and in communities—is that working people will then *demand* those things, not just as individuals but as part of the mass movement that Sanders constantly argues for.

They're starting to demand them, as we are seeing in the teachers' strike wave that has swept the country from West Virginia, Oklahoma, and Arizona, to California and Chicago and far beyond, even into the anti-union charter-school sector.

Graduate workers and faculty are striking in increasing numbers in higher education, everywhere from elite universities like Harvard, where graduate workers voted to authorize a strike at the time of this writing, to community colleges in Chicago, where faculty struck in May 2019.

That strike wave hasn't yet fully arrived in the private sector, but there are hopeful signs: the United Auto Workers undertook a long, grueling strike at General Motors beginning in September 2019, wringing some concessions out of the company. The Communications Workers of America and the hospitality workers' union UNITE HERE have long been outliers in their repeated willingness to strike, respectively, against communications giant Verizon and hotel chains like Hyatt and Hilton. Health workers like nurses have also become strike happy across multiple unions in for-profit and nonprofit hospitals and other health institutions throughout the country.

And who could forget the immortal words of Association of Flight Attendants president Sara Nelson, whose union's threat of a strike, along with other airport workers' actions like air traffic controllers calling in sick en masse, led to an end to Donald Trump's government shutdown in late 2018 and early 2019? "Strike, strike, strike, strike, strike, strike, strike," she told a labor historian. "Say it—it feels good."

Sanders himself isn't solely responsible for this militancy, of course—his message of higher expectations and the necessity of struggle to win gains is only having mass resonance because decades of worsening conditions for the working class have made people ready to hear it. Stagnant wages, rising rents, attacks on pensions, a dramatic decline in workplace democracy, and a rising sense of precarity and hopelessness are only some of the many miseries facing workers in the twenty-first century. But objectively bad conditions aren't enough to spur working people to action. They also need a change in their *subjective* sense of agency, a sense that if they act collectively, they can actually change the terrible conditions they find themselves in. Sanders's campaigns have contributed to a rise in working-class militancy throughout the country by helping give workers a sense of their power.

It probably won't surprise you to hear that socialists are thrilled to see a new working-class upsurge potentially emerging after decades of decline for the labor movement. But we aren't just cheering from the sidelines. Socialists are joining those fights and helping rebuild the labor movement.

How Not to Rebuild Labor

Before talking about how to revive labor and the work socialists are already doing to help, we should talk about how *not* to do it. Given the importance of the labor movement in winning progressive change, many labor scholars, academics, lawyers, and organizers have put forward plans to revitalize the labor movement during its period of decline.

Most proposed solutions fall into three categories: (1) policy fixes, especially labor law reform like the Employee Free Choice Act that would make it easier to form unions—a law unions desperately hoped President Barack Obama would pass during his tenure in office but did not; (2) campaign strategy fixes, such as the employment of "corporate campaigns" that many unions now use as a means to pressure bosses through the targeting of large institutional investors in a company or releasing information that could hurt a company's stock price; and (3) electoral fixes, including the election of sympathetic politicians, almost entirely from the

Democratic Party, and pressure on politicians to pass reforms like minimum wage hikes.

If implemented, all of these proposals would certainly help rebuild worker power. The problem is, these ideas of union revitalization all imagine that process coming from above, whether by lawmakers, lawyers, or union staff and leadership. But effective unions fundamentally draw their power from below, through organizing and mobilizing workers at the workplace and engaging in militant actions like strikes.

The periods that saw the largest upsurge in worker power—in the private sector in the 1930s and '40s and the public sector in the 1960s and '70s—were characterized by massive social mobilizations and strike waves in workplaces across the country that created crises to which elites had to respond. When public-sector workers like teachers, postal workers, and many others went on illegal strikes in the '60s and '70s, many union leaders were thrown in jail—postal workers even saw President Richard Nixon send in the National Guard to try to sort the mail during their national illegal strike in 1970. But the disruptions these workers caused led reluctant politicians to make changes in the law that provided workers with basic union rights.

After the militant upsurges of the 1930s, political scientist Michael Goldfield writes, "the labor insurgency, with its accompanying conflict and violence caused by intransigent company resistance, had reached proportions truly alarming to the economic and political elites." On May 29, 1934, one member of the House of Representatives argued breathlessly, "You have seen strikes in Toledo, you have seen Minneapolis, you have seen San Francisco, and you have seen some of the southern textile strikes . . . but . . . you have not yet seen the gates of hell opened, and that is what is going to happen from now on." Rather than allow those gates to be thrown open, the Democratic Party led the charge to give American workers major concessions.

The gains for unions in members, wages and benefits, and power on the job didn't come principally because someone at the top opened the door for workers to organize. They came as a result of upsurges driven forward by an empowered rank and file, often with unions whose leaders understood the necessity of such empowerment. At both the rank-and-file and leadership level, socialists played key roles in those upsurges.

The Militant Minority

These insurgent movements were based in the workplace and relied on workers joining together, withholding their labor, and forcibly extracting concessions from their bosses and governments. The most successful unions were led by, and based in, the "militant minority," a dedicated layer of activists in the workplace who were recognized as leaders by their coworkers and who advanced a class-struggle approach to their organizing—an understanding that winning required organizing their coworkers to fight the bosses. They were the most respected workers, the hardest fighters, the most dedicated organizers, and the ones that most actively built unions' cultures of solidarity. Historically, leftists—socialists, Communists, Trotskyists, anarchists, and others—played a key (though far from the only) role within this militant minority that drove the union movement forward.

Today's labor movement largely lacks a militant minority, at least in numbers large enough to turn the tide in workers' favor. Rebuilding this class-conscious, combative layer of workers in workplaces is central to reviving the trade unions, and must be a central task for the rising socialist movement.

The militant minority made the key difference in many unions that successfully took on the corporate oligarchs during the Great Depression and New Deal era, and helped some unions buck the tide of conservatism and bureaucratization that labor experienced during and after World War II.

Who made up this militant minority? The composition varied depending on location and industry. In the United Packinghouse Workers of America, for instance, in cities like Chicago, black workers composed an important segment, pushing the UPWA to adopt a broad "social unionism" that didn't just fight for better pay and working conditions, but also took on white supremacy. Elsewhere in UPWA locals, in places like Kansas City and rural Minnesota, class-conscious white ethnics played a key role. But the groups who played the most important role in forming and maintaining strong class-struggle unions were socialists of one kind or another who held explicit political commitments to militant unionism.

While these radicals have played key roles throughout American labor history, they achieved the most in the lead-up to and heyday of the Congress of Industrial Organizations (CIO). The United States had seen previous periods of labor upsurge. But the upsurge of the Great Depression/New Deal and World War II eras coincided with an era of strong leftist organizations of various types in workplaces around the country. The particular strand of radical left organization that was dominant varied depending on the given union or industry or region, but the Communist Party proved the most influential during industrial unions' formative years, constituting what sociologists Judith Stepan-Norris and Maurice Zeitlin call "the main expression of native, working-class radicalism in the United States."

What did these socialist members of the militant minority do? Their left ideology spurred them to promote class struggle rather than class snuggle with management, both on shop-floor issues as well as broader fightbacks. They were often labor's most seasoned, dedicated organizers. They served as a link between workplace and community struggles. They were the most active day-to-day builders of the unions and its activities. And they often helped lead their unions, either from the shop floor or union office—and ideally from both.

This militant minority layer unfortunately declined in the labor movement—and with it, the link between the Left and labor was severed. This problem still plagues the socialist movement today. The decline came as a result of many injuries, some self-inflicted, others from without. Most important was the postwar Red Scare that drove Communists from unions and radicalism from much of the American body politic. The 1947 Taft-Hartley Act required unions to enforce a no-Communist pledge, leading to the expulsion of radical unionists and blacklisting of Communist- and other socialist-led unions. Many liberal union leaders also saw in these purges an opportunity to rid their unions of their most strident critics. The result was a massive purging of labor's strongest organizers and leaders who not only led workers out on strike but also encouraged unions to fight racism and other forms of oppression through the union itself.

But the Left itself was not blameless. Because of their fealty to the often erratic party line that was handed down to them from Moscow, the Communist Party made a number of key errors during and after World War II that alienated it from the rank and file it had helped organize. The party's wild shifts in strategy hurt it in the eyes of many workers, many of whom had long respected their Communist fellow workers for their incredible dedication to rank-and-file organizing. The shifts were sudden, contradictory, and related little to workers' struggles on the job. Workers outside the party were understandably suspicious. Additionally, soon after playing key roles at the rank-and-file level in the working-class upsurges of the 1930s, the Communist Party shifted its orientation toward permeating the new CIO union bureaucracy and the Democratic Party, aiming to ingratiate itself to political and labor power brokers rather than build independent shop-floor power. This reorientation essentially meant that the party was not in a position to seriously defend itself against the postwar onslaught.

The success of the postwar Red Scare in purging radicals helped cut the connection between socialists and the working class. Without union leaders, organizers, and rank-and-filers committed to what labor writer and organizer Jane McAlevey calls "whole worker organizing" (another term for "social unionism," in which unionists fought not just for themselves but for the broader communities they were embedded in), the unions came to be seen by many as just another "interest group" fighting on behalf of its members. Despite a renewed interest in socialism in the 1960s and '70s, the new generation of radicals remained largely disconnected from unions and the workplace—and the noble and heroic efforts of some labor-oriented activists to overcome this gap were insufficient to rebuild a cohesive militant minority capable of transforming the labor movement.

Rebuilding the Militant Minority

Why does all of this history matter? Because if labor is to pick itself back up, organizing the overwhelming numbers of unorganized workers in the country and striking in mass numbers to again become a working-class force to be reckoned with, rebuilding a militant minority will be key. And past experience—as well as recent cases of successful labor action—strongly suggests that socialists will be essential to rebuilding that layer. The best strategy for doing so, as well as for ending the severed link between the working class and the Left, is called the rank-and-file strategy, which focuses on identifying, developing, and expanding the layer of workplace leaders who are primed to fight the boss—and embedding socialists within those fights.

The rank-and-file strategy is fundamentally about winning socialism. If the working class is the key agent of change to win socialism, then the only way to get there is to expand the number of class-conscious worker organizers and activists—and rooting the socialist movement in this layer. Given the enforced decades-long divorce of socialists from the working class, reconnecting labor and Left is a particularly urgent task.

The tactics of the rank-and-file strategy, as well as some of the key parts of the analysis informing those tactics, have been around since the heyday of the early Communist Party in the 1920s. One of the principal tactics involves radicals focusing their political work within industries that have a strategic position in the American economy and society. In the 1920s and '30s, socialists were often already employed in these jobs, but in today's context, socialists often will have to more pro-actively search for work in a strategic location.

"Strategic" can be defined broadly: during the mid-twentieth century, for example, radicals carrying out a version of this strategy often worked in steel or auto manufacturing, given how central those industries were to the American economy at the time. Radicals looking for a similarly key node of the US economy today might choose the logistics sector, including shipping and warehouse work. Or radicals could choose to become educators, given how transformative the recent wave of teachers' strikes has been; or nurses or other health workers, given both the growing importance of the health sector in the American economy and the importance of getting health workers to join the fight for Medicare for All. Defining what's strategic is as much an art as a science, and varies depending on context.

As is suggested by its name, the rank-and-file strategy is largely oriented to building power at the workplace level—as opposed to, say, carrying out support campaigns for already existing unions from the outside or permeating the existing union officialdom. Achieving this goal often means organizing to boot out conservative old guards in the unions and electing in their place militants committed to developing an empowered rank and file—and accountable to that same layer.

Part of this bottom-up orientation comes from an analysis of the nature of union bureaucracies. Radicals have long recognized that workers' potential power on the job and willingness to engage in militant action frequently comes up against conservative pressures exerted by full-time labor officials. Successful unions need full-time leaders and staffers, of course—you can't run unions without people whose job is to process union dues or send out fliers for meetings or keep the lights on at the union hall. The problem is that those officials face a distinct set of incentives and pressures that are separate from those of workers.

By being elected or chosen to be part of union staff, workers who once toiled on brutal assembly lines or in front of classrooms of screaming children now hold more comfortable positions, get to work in a comfortable office, gain influence and power as union leaders among their former coworkers and perhaps local or national politicians, and often make more money than they did when working their old job. What's more, they're also tasked with administering the massive holdings of the union, which in the United States often includes pension funds, health care plans, real estate holdings, and more.

Even the best-intentioned leaders are often reluctant to promote risky actions like strikes or other kinds of militant action—the very source of workers' power. This is particularly true in a country like the United States where corporations are particularly strong and labor rights are extremely weak. Effective strikes in either the public or private sector often risk being punished with massive fines or even jail time for union leaders.

Eric Blanc writes about this dynamic at length in his chronicle of the teachers' strike wave that began in 2018, *Red State Revolt*. Repeatedly, in the illegal strikes that kicked off in West Virginia, Oklahoma, and Arizona, the official union leaderships were reluctant to engage in militant action. In West Virginia, for example, where the strike wave started, rank-and-file teachers had started to organize what would eventually become a strike through social media. On January 23, 2018, in Mingo County, West Virginia, 250 teachers gathered to discuss a possible strike action. Two union staffers told the room that the state's union leadership was against an immediate strike. Workers immediately pushed back, insisting they set a date for a statewide strike. The staffers soon backed off.

"Who am I to argue with an entire county of workers?" asked one. "At least 90 percent wanted to walk out. One lady stood up and said to us, 'Listen you all can either get behind us or get out of the way, because if you don't, we'll run you over.'"

Of course, it's not just as simple as "rank-and-file workers good, union leaders bad." It would be simplistic and absurd to argue that the rank and file is rip-roaring ready to strike, only to be held back by the dastardly bureaucrats. Most of the time, workers *aren't* activated and excited about taking militant action. But union leaders all too often perpetuate this state of resignation and even push back against incipient efforts from below to take on the bosses.

Though most union leaders want to see their members' lives improved and worker power grow, they all face structural pressures that pull them toward conservatism. That's why simply electing new leaders is insufficient—without a conscious and empowered rank and file, even the best individual leaders will tend to cave in the face of immense pressures from above.

Many union officials aren't just conservative when it comes to interacting with their own members; they also make conservative decisions when it comes to politics more generally. Their behavior during the 2016 election showed this perfectly. Despite the fact that Bernie Sanders was the most pro-worker major American presidential candidate in generations, very few unions endorsed him. In fact, documents released by WikiLeaks ahead of the 2016 election showed that the American Federation of Teachers president Randi Weingarten not only engineered an early endorsement from her union for Hillary Clinton rather than Bernie, but promised to "go after" another union, National Nurses United, for its Sanders endorsement. Another president, Tom Buffenbarger of the

International Association of Machinists and Aerospace Workers, actually appeared to rig his union's endorsement vote to ensure Clinton would get the nomination.

Acting as supplicants for a Democratic Party that has given them very little over the years, moving further and further away from a politics that benefits unions and workers in general, most of the labor bureaucracy in the United States currently acts as a barrier not just to waging class struggle in the workplace but to campaigning in class-struggle elections outside it with the backing of the labor movement. The Sanders campaigns have helped cohere a group of union activists around the group Labor for Bernie who have agitated for their local and international unions to endorse Sanders. Groups like Labor for Bernie could act as a nucleus around which left-wing unionists can come together, as part of a broader class-struggle current in the movement, to push labor to embrace a different kind of electoral politics than the one that has failed for so long.

Leadership Struggles

A key piece of the rank-and-file strategy involves challenging conservatism and resignation at a shop-floor level—and it often also means organizing with other rank-and-file members to run for leadership in those unions where a conservative union bureaucracy refuses to fight the boss.

Taking over union leadership is far from a be-all, end-all tactic of the rank-and-file strategy. In fact, doing so without leaning on or building an empowered layer of workplace leaders can end in complete disaster. But a number of the most inspiring, successful, and militant strikes of the last few decades have been waged and won precisely because socialists, working with other non-socialist members of the militant minority, formed internal reform caucuses within their unions, wrested leadership away from the old guard, and transformed their unions into vehicles to fight not just their own capitalist bosses but *for* the entire working class. They re-formed that militant minority layer on the job, translated the power they built on the shop floor into taking over the union leadership, and led broad struggles on behalf of the entire working class through that union.

For example, a group of rank-and-file reformers within the notoriously corrupt Teamsters union began organizing in the 1970s through a group called Teamsters for a Democratic Union. Some of TDU's founders were socialists, most of them from a now-defunct group called the International Socialists. But the reform movement they built within the union was overwhelmingly non-socialist. They were pissed-off truckers, UPS drivers, and other members who were sick of being members of an undemocratic, ineffectual, and crooked union.

After years of organizing within the union, TDU's big break came in 1991, when after successfully convincing government overseers of a campaign to root out corruption in the union to hold the first democratic election to elect the Teamsters president in the union's history, a TDU-backed reform candidate named Ron Carey won the union's presidency. Carey quickly got to work, selling off its two private jets, cutting his salary by a third, and cleaning house of dozens of corrupt Teamsters officials. Most importantly, he led UPS workers in a massive nationwide strike in 1997, taking on one of the world's largest corporations through militant action and framing the problems those drivers were up against at work, like the prevalence of part-time jobs in the company, as the problems of the entire American working class. The strike's slogan was "Part-Time America Won't Work." Incredibly, the

Teamsters won the strike. After two decades of beatdowns and losses in most major union fights, it seemed that the victorious UPS strike might be the spark to reverse labor's fortunes.

Eventually the old guard drove Carey out of the union, leveling corruption charges against him that were ultimately proven false. But what remains is the example of a successful, militant, nationwide strike in the private sector supported by the American public—and the socialists who carried out the rank-and-file strategy helped make it possible. Many of them are still organizing within TDU; others still organize around the union reform organization Labor Notes.

The Chicago Teachers Union presents a similar example of a successful rank-and-file upsurge that took over and transformed its union. The CTU drew international attention for waging a successful strike against neoliberal Democratic villain extraordinaire, Mayor Rahm Emanuel, in 2012. The strike came at a time when public education and teachers in particular were under attack by education privatizers (including within the Democratic Party), unions had won few major victories in years, austerity was vicious, and the mayor was hell-bent on destroying the CTU. Instead, the seven-day strike completely transformed the city, drawing tens of thousands of teachers to massive rallies in downtown Chicago, terrible press for Emanuel and the privatizers, and, according to multiple polls during the strike, the overwhelming support of Chicago's working class—the very people who were massively inconvenienced by the teachers walking out and who had to scramble to figure out where to send their kids.

The strike became a beacon in Chicago and around the country. It inspired education workers at charter schools, universities, and community colleges throughout the city to strike in the years to come; teachers in "red states" like West Virginia and "blue states" like California closely studied the lessons of Chicago in organizing for their own strikes in 2018 and 2019. None of it would have been possible without a group of teachers, some socialists but mostly not, organizing together throughout the 2000s to force their conservative union leadership to join the fight already underway in the city against education austerity, led by community groups in neighborhoods of color in the city's working-class neighborhoods.

The reformers, who created a reform caucus called the Caucus of Rank-and-File Educators (CORE), couldn't have led the union out on strike without first running for union leadership in 2010 and winning. They, too, immediately began transforming their union, slashing bloated salaries at the top and creating a new organizing department to educate and engage their members to prepare for a strike as well as organize alongside community groups. They remade the CTU, waged a successful strike, inspired teachers and other workers around the country to learn from and improve upon their model, and planted a flag for democratic, militant unionism that fought for the entire working class, especially against the racial inequalities in the Chicago school system. And they did so by carrying out the rank-and-file strategy.

The union struck twice in the years after 2012, going on an illegal one-day political strike that focused specifically on raising revenue in Chicago and the state of Illinois by taxing the rich, and striking in 2019 for two full weeks for smaller class sizes and desperately needed additional social workers, nurses, and librarians; they struck alongside another union, SEIU Local 73, that represented the low-wage school staff. The union has experienced its ups and downs since CORE's victory, including crushing defeats like Emanuel's closing of forty-nine schools in the city, but it has also become the most powerful progressive political force in the city, the axis around which the broader left-labor movement in Chicago—including the socialist and progressive electoral successes we wrote about in chapter 3—turns.

One of the groups of workers CTU helped inspire was West Virginia teachers. In the summer of 2017, in the wake of the Bernie Sanders campaign and the election of Trump, teachers Emily Comer and Jay O'Neal met in a study group of labor strategist and organizer Jane McAlevey's book *No Shortcuts*, organized by the newly formed chapter of the Democratic Socialists of America in Charleston. Over the following months they founded a Facebook group for public employees that became a central organizing tool and went on to organize with other teachers in the state who weren't DSA members or radicals of any kind to fight low pay and attacks on their health care. Their efforts helped kick off the West Virginia teachers' strike, which in turn ignited the current teachers' strike wave, the biggest strike upsurge the United States has seen in forty years.

The kind of reinvigoration and reorganization that new, radical leadership can bring to unions can form the basis for organizing the masses of unorganized workers. In Chicago, for example, the CTU has not only gone on strike for itself, but also carried out huge organizing drives in charter schools in the city, inspiring a smaller teachers' strike wave within the city's charter sector. Unions that are transformed into democratic, militant organizations that fight for the entire working class can serve as a beacon to unorganized workers, showing them how union membership can transform the world.

Socialists and the Rank-and-File Strategy

At its 2019 national convention, DSA passed a measure adopting the rank-and-file strategy as part of its approach to labor work. Unsurprisingly, that strategy quickly came under fire by some sections of the union officialdom, including in New York City where, as *Politico* reported, the city's DSA branch had already developed a plan in which its members would take jobs that would allow them to join important unions and help transform them. One city union leader accused DSA of "sow[ing] the seeds of disunity by targeting some of the most progressive unions in our city with plans for infiltration and disruption." Such leaders don't take kindly to challenges to their power from anyone, and are happy to paint challengers as dangerous radicals descending upon the union to carry out a devious agenda. But the entire point of the rank-and-file strategy is for radicals not to approach workers' struggles from the outside, but actually wage them as members of the union, fighting alongside other workers in solidarity with them.

And what's so devious about the plan, anyway? Socialists need jobs just like everyone else, and our job prospects are just as bleak as everyone else's. Radicals generally aren't giving up cushy careers in academia or well-paid, low-impact jobs in the private sector; those jobs largely don't exist in the twenty-first century, and are becoming rarer by the day. Many socialists currently work in jobs that pay too little, are meaningless or tedious, and lack union protection. It makes sense for them to get union jobs both as socialists *and* as workers.

Many DSA members are currently doing this. Jill Young, a member of Indianapolis DSA who is twenty-nine, chose to go into the building trades. She took a job in 2019 as a millwright's apprentice with Millwrights Local Union 1076. A millwright is a construction mechanic who installs, maintains, and dismantles machinery like conveyor systems, turbine engines for wind and gas, and robotics. Young describes her decision this way:

> Economically and on a personal level, joining a union was a no-brainer. As a first-year apprentice my paychecks are bigger than at my previous job I'd held for years and which was in my field of study in college . . . Taking a union job has opened up possibilities to me that seem basic and essential, but which were unattainable to me before: not living paycheck to paycheck, not panicking over unexpected vet and car bills, the ability to seriously consider the costs of a wedding. For the first time, I can realistically imagine myself paying off my student loans, buying a home, having a family.
>
> On a grander scale, my decision to join a union was influenced by my belief in the power of organized labor to secure a better life for working-class people, and the dire need to revitalize the American labor movement. The changes we need to wrest economic and political power away from the wealthy, to decommodify necessities like health care and housing, and to save the planet from climate change will not come without a strong labor movement capable of withholding labor and winning demands. I don't think there's a better way to do my part in this fight than to be an active rank-and-file member of a union with sights set on broad, class-wide demands.

Molly Armstrong, a twenty-nine-year-old member of DSA who lives in Northern California, identifies the same two factors in her decision to go to nursing school: economic stability and a broader sense of political purpose, informed by her experiences as a socialist. She explains,

> For a while I was working in nonprofits, and was growing disillusioned with them. I was paying over half my income to rent, and I couldn't save enough money to have a stable financial future. I was surrounded by brilliant, thoughtful, kind people who I saw as being like Sisyphus, rolling giant stones up the mountain only to have them roll down again. It all just seemed pointless.
>
> I had gone into that line of work because before that I had been a personal assistant and nanny to a family of billionaires, and I was so disturbed by that egregious wealth. I thought that nonprofits were the way to do good in the world. But the irony was that in the nonprofit world, you just end up trying to curry favor with those same people anyway. When Bernie Sanders ran for president, I started to understand why I had become disillusioned. Nonprofits weren't actually redefining the power structures in our society.
>
> The day Trump won was the day I decided to join DSA. I had quit my nonprofit job and was doing odd jobs— babysitting, walking dogs, doing personal assistant work, you name it. When I started organizing with DSA I finally came to understand what the labor movement was. My mom's a teacher, but growing up I can't remember ever hearing about unions. Through the organizing and political education I was doing and the conversations I was having in DSA, I started to see that all of those things that bothered me in the other workplaces could be different with a union.

I began to understand for the first time the idea of working-class solidarity. Instead of negotiating for a raise in secret in competition with your coworkers, instead of brown-nosing and currying favor with the people in power, we unite to demand something from those people in power together. And so I decided to go to nursing school and become a unionized nurse.

I didn't decide this in a vacuum. I remember having a meeting with two other DSA members who were in a similar situation: no appealing job prospects and a growing understanding of class struggle and commitment to social-ism. We connected with some older people in DSA who had become rank-and-file union activists in the 1970s and '80s, and realized that if we did this, we would be carrying on a proud tradition. It felt exciting, and like we were part of something so much bigger. One of them is now in nursing school with me, and the other is becoming a union teacher.

For years I had a pit in my stomach. Shouldn't I be more fulfilled, happier? Since deciding to go to nursing school I haven't felt that. Everything is confirmed for me that this is the right thing, over and over. We're all taught that the way to be fulfilled is to be unique and get ahead by yourself, but what's really fulfilling is solidarity. We all have our special talents, but we can use those talents to bolster each other and rise together. I was taught that in DSA.

Armstrong's fellow DSA member and nursing student Ari Marcantonio said much the same:

When Bernie Sanders ran for president in 2016 he opened my eyes to the possibility of a different world. I realized that, in the richest country in history, there was no reason we couldn't guarantee health care, housing, education, and a good job to every person. I began to realize that the fact that so many go without the basic necessities of life isn't an accident but a result of billionaires paying low wages, evading taxes, and destroying the environment. I began to understand that exploitation is core to capitalism, but I also began to see a path to a different world. I learned about the struggles that had won things I took for granted, things like the eight-hour work day, child labor laws, and unemployment insurance. I saw what collective action could achieve and came to understand that the only way progress had ever been made was when the working class stood together to demand it.

I went to a meeting of the Democratic Socialists of America. I quickly became a highly involved member of the organization, which grew dramatically during this time. The education I received as a member of the DSA was the best of my life. I grew politically, as an organizer, and came to see myself as part of a socialist and workers' movement that had been fighting for a better world for hundreds of years.

At this point I had never had a very good job. I had worked in restaurants, art galleries, and as a freelancer writing marketing materials. I had thought for a while that I would take a job as a labor organizer but was troubled by what I had come to understand about the state of unions in America. Most are bureaucratic, top down, and actively opposed to workers taking initiative.

It was during this time that I read more about the history of American labor. I read about the Great Steel Strike of 1919, the sit-downs in Akron's rubber factories, the general strike that brought the ruling class of Minneapolis to its knees and paved the way for the unionization of that city. I read about ordinary men and women who accomplished extraordinary feats, organizing their coworkers to take on the most powerful forces on earth. I could see no force more powerful than militant and democratic unions, organized from the bottom up by shop-floor activists, and I knew then that this was the place for me to be.

If we're going to win a better world, rebuilding the labor movement (and the militant minority within it) will be essential. We'll need many more people heading into the labor movement planning to be dedicated organizers, like those quoted above, to do it.

A Strong Dose of Socialist Humility

Rebuilding the labor movement won't happen solely through the efforts of socialists, of course—it never has. Socialists have a particular set of organizing tactics and strategies that aim to widen the scope of class struggle as much as possible, rooted in a worldview that sees workers as capable of not just winning gains for themselves but transforming the entire world. But we shouldn't be arrogant about what we bring to the table, especially since we know a lot less about organizing to win working-class power than we should—and because it usually takes a considerable amount of time to learn how to do a job right and garner the respect of your coworkers. Longtime labor activist and Labor Notes cofounder Kim Moody puts it this way:

> Socialists are not active in the unions or other working-class organizations simply to recruit or propagandize. The first

task is to build the broader movement . . . Socialists . . . have a great many positions on a great many things . . . But engaging workplace conflict with some prepackaged "program" of demands not only reeks of arrogance, but is bound to prove irrelevant to workers who already understand their grievances perfectly well . . . In the fight for better conditions, with workers in motion, other ("bigger") issues will emerge. But it is the existing issues and struggles that are the starting point.

We think our ideas are good ones—otherwise we wouldn't be socialists. But we won't win without working hand in hand with people who aren't socialists, and we won't win anyone over to our politics by acting like leftist missionaries or jerks.

The history of socialists in the US labor movement suggests that we can do movement work with the kind of humility counseled by Moody. If we do, who knows what kind of beautiful world we can win together?

Labor Notes is the most important project in the United States dedicated to rebuild that militant minority layer, encouraging union militancy and democracy, and training rank-and-file workers to be effective shop-floor fighters and connecting them with other such fighters across geography and industry. Socialists were the ones who founded Labor Notes in 1979, but if you go to one of their national conferences or regional "Troublemakers Schools" that they regularly put on, you won't see a room full of members of socialist organizations. Some participants through their workplace activism have come to socialist politics; most probably haven't. But all have been shaped by ideas about union militancy and democracy that socialists in joint struggle with nonsocialists have put forward. Through that struggle, they've worked to organize exactly the layer of militant workers that we'll need to rebuild the labor movement.

For the Common Good

Socialists and the other class-conscious members of the militant minority bring much to labor struggles. Whereas many union leaders don't want to engage in strikes and other forms of labor militancy, opting to cut deals with management instead of building power on the shop floor, socialists argue that worker power comes from walking off the job and building a fightback that benefits the entire working class. Whereas those same leaders often worry about running unions democratically, fearing that an empowered and active rank and file could threaten their power as leaders, socialists want fully democratic unions. We also argue for unions to fight for the entire working class, not just their members.

All workers need unions, and it's always better to have one at your job than not have one—they give you a modicum of democracy on the job, and on average union workers have 12 percent higher wages than nonunion workers. But unions aren't inherently progressive. At worst, they can be used for openly reactionary purposes. Building trades unions like those for plumbers and carpenters, for example, have a long history of trying to exclude workers of color from joining. Numerous union leaders affiliated with extractive industries like oil have come out against a Green New Deal and efforts to wean our planet off fossil fuels. Members of the AFL-CIO's Energy Committee wrote a letter to Representative Ocasio-Cortez and Senator Ed Markey, the original sponsors of the Green New Deal proposal, that it "makes promises that are not achievable or realistic." And while most unions aren't outright reactionary, they often keep their agenda limited to improving wages and benefits for their members.

But organized labor has incredible power in society that can be used to fight for far more than wages and benefits. A number of unions have taken up a strategy called "bargaining for the common good," in which they fight not just for policies that benefit them but for the entire working class. And socialists have a long history of leading exactly that kind of unionism.

Bargaining for the common good is most obvious in the public sector or in industries like health care, where the interests of union workers and service users often line up closely alongside one another. The Chicago Teachers Union has led the way in recent years, using its contract fights and political power during elections to fight for "the schools Chicago's children deserve," affordable housing in a rapidly gentrifying city, and other low-wage workers like bus drivers and classroom aides, as well as against racial inequality in the school system, police brutality in the city as a whole, and public money giveaways to corporations. Similarly, health care unions have fought for—and, in California, won—minimum nurse-to-patient ratios that aim to prevent hospital management from overloading nurses with more patients than they can properly care for, a policy that benefits both patients and nurses.

Part of what made the 2018 West Virginia teachers' strike so powerful was that its final settlement included raises of 5 percent for *all* public employees in the state, not just educators. The roots of that wide-ranging raise were in the teacher organizers' decision to include all public employees in the West Virginia Facebook group that was the principal site of organizing for the strike.

Similarly, teachers Emily Comer and Jay O'Neal were the ones who brought the question of progressive taxation in West Virginia to the fore during the strike, arguing that was the only way to deal with the problems of the state health care program, administered through the Public Employees Insurance Agency. In one online post, O'Neal wrote: "By the time of the work stoppage, the idea that PEIA should be fixed by increasing the gas severance tax [on the state's large natural gas mining industry] prevailed among public employees. During the nine school days of the strike, chants of 'Tax our gas!' periodically erupted inside the capital."

In the public sector, it's difficult for unions to win without adopting this "bargaining for the common good" approach. When teachers or nurses walk off the job, they're not leaving widgets on the assembly line like autoworkers do—they're ending provision of a desperately needed social good, like teaching children or caring for sick patients.

To win such strikes, they need to make the case to those service users and the public as a whole that they're walking off the job to *strengthen* those services, not just win a better deal for themselves—otherwise elected officials can easily divide them from the rest of the working class that relies on those services and are themselves suffering under austerity, as happened with public school teachers in New York City and black and brown parents and community members during and in the wake of the bitter Ocean Hill–Brownsville teachers' strikes of 1968 over issues of community control in schools. By walking off the job without standing shoulder to shoulder with community members, both the largely white workforce of teachers and communities of color they taught in ended up losing, for decades.

The bargaining for the common good approach is more difficult in the private sector, but it's not impossible, as the Teamsters' 1997 UPS strike showed.

Socialists didn't invent this approach and aren't the only ones who argue for it. Most of the members of the Chicago Teachers Union who went on strike for better schools for Chicago's students weren't socialists. Neither were most West Virginia teachers or UPS drivers. But it's an approach that socialists have always fought for, and that must be central to our labor strategy going forward.

A Class-Struggle Approach to Winning a Green New Deal
Adopting a rank-and-file–led, class-struggle approach to our work in the labor movement isn't just essential for revitalizing the labor movement—it's also necessary for winning fights that are usually thought of as outside labor's purview. We argued earlier in this book for the absolute necessity of winning a Green New Deal. The best way to win it is through a class-struggle approach. Several ecosocialists in DSA, writing in its publication *Socialist Forum*, framed such an approach this way:

> Winning a transformative GND will require massive leverage over the political and economic system. We need the ability to force these changes over the objection of broad sections of the capitalist class, who are fiercely unwilling to lose their profits. The confrontational tactics and electoral challenges of the growing GND movement are essential parts of the leverage we need, but we think history shows they won't be enough. We will also need direct leverage against the capitalist class, right in the places where they make their money. Who has that leverage? In short, working people, united and organized.

This goes back to our previous argument about why socialists focus so much on workers: workers, because they are positioned at the very heart of the capitalist system, producing the profits that the capitalists who run our society care so much about, possess incredible power. We'll need them to use it to save the planet.

Part of a class-struggle approach includes what the GND is already doing, like advancing proposals that benefit rather than hurt workers in extractive industries. But it also has to include a strategy for winning buy-in for the GND from the working-class movement itself. Unions need to get on board for a GND. A few have already taken steps in the right direction: the Service Employees International Union has passed a resolution endorsing the GND, and several American Federation of Teachers locals have endorsed it, while the international union has joined climate protests in support of it. These are necessary first steps to throwing labor's full weight behind the proposal. But the heavier lift will be convincing workers in the extractive and basic infrastructure industries like the building trades, oil workers, and coal miners.

We might assume that such unions are always going to be resolutely opposed to such action. Indeed, currently, most are. The AFL-CIO's Energy Committee passed an aforementioned resolution in 2019 decrying the GND; a group of building trades union officials actually met with Donald Trump shortly after he took office and posed for pictures with him, all smiles. Key trade union officials have been on the wrong side of many of the most important environmental battles of recent years, including the Keystone XL pipeline fight.

Clearly, moving these unions from strongly defending environmental destruction to becoming key protagonists in stopping it will require a lot of work. We might be tempted to believe that given how these workers currently benefit from climate destruction, convincing them to join us is impossible. But history shows us it's not.

Labor historian Trish Kahle has written at length about environmentalism and the United Mine Workers (UMW) of America, a coal miners' union that represents a paradigmatic dirty-energy industry. Coal is one of the dirtiest sources of energy we have, one that must be phased out as soon as possible in the transition to clean energy. Donald Trump also heavily courted coal miners in his 2016 election campaign, promising that coal jobs would return to devastated former coal mining communities and even donning a hard hat and his best tough-guy-coal-miner face at one of his campaign rallies in coal country.

Coal miners who have seen their livelihoods devastated as we transition away from coal are perhaps understandably susceptible to such appeals from the Right. But Kahle shows that they don't have to be—and weren't, even in the 1960s and '70s, when a rank-and-file reform movement, Miners for Democracy, demanded not only democratic and militant unionism in the coal fields, but an environmental transformation of their work.

"Every union should have a vision of the future," stated Jock Yablonski, the progressive union leader who ran to be UMW president in 1969. "What good is a union that reduces coal dust in the mines only to have miners and their families breathe pollutants in the air, drink pollutants in the water, and eat contaminated commodities?"

Yablonski was later murdered by thugs hired by the corrupt union incumbent he sought to replace, a tragedy documented in Barbara Kopple's classic documentary *Harlan County, USA*.

But Miners for Democracy (MFD) was formed in the year after his death, its original membership made up of Yablonski's supporters. It proceeded to argue for an end to the most environmentally destructive forms of coal mining.

"The MFD shifted the terms of the debate. Instead of a choice between jobs and environment, they argued for different priorities: people and land before profit. In fact, the MFD said that investing in the environment was the best way to protect jobs," Kahle writes. The rank-and-file miners argued that the UMW "must become the most progressive force in the region," advocating not only for workers but the broader communities in which they lived and the planet as a whole—the "bargaining for the common good" approach we mentioned above. The example of the MFD within the UMW shows that even in the dirtiest of industries, it is possible to win workers over to an environmentally sustainable future.

Taking a class-struggle approach to winning a GND doesn't just mean getting unions to back it. It also means ensuring workers make radical demands and take direct action to win those demands. What could that look like? In August 2019, a group of Northern Ireland shipyard workers, having heard that their shipyard's parent company planned to close the yard, responded by occupying it, demanding that the UK government nationalize it and switch production to green energy. Their union spokesperson told a journalist during the occupation, "There's massive potential in wind turbines and tidal energy. They're saying they could create thousands of jobs, and that we need a just transition to renewable energy." Activists involved in the shutdown said they were inspired by Alexandria Ocasio-Cortez's Green New Deal plan.

Some German unions, too, have recently joined the fight, including in the trades. IG Metall, the country's metalworkers' union and the largest union in Germany, has begun organizing demonstrations demanding a green transition as well as on-the-job actions and education; the German transport workers' union and ver.di, the country's second-largest union, has also joined.

If unions are going to come around to support the GND, rank-and-file radicals will have to play key roles within those unions, especially within unions working in the infrastructure and extraction industries. These should be seen as strategic industries for socialists to get jobs and organize in, since the task to reverse these unions' stances on climate change—and of convincing workers to disrupt business as usual in order to force meaningful change—is the most urgent task we currently face as a species.

A Workers' World to Win

Workers have both the power and the self-interest to fight for a better world, the world that socialists want to win. Currently, socialists aren't embedded in working-class struggles the way we need to be to win that world. That has to change. Luckily, many in the burgeoning socialist movement in the United States realize that and are joining the fights at the rank-and-file level. But we have to make that movement a lot bigger.

Without a rank-and-file revolution, the kind of political revolution Bernie Sanders has talked so much about won't come to pass. Taxing the rich, winning Medicare for All or a Green New Deal—none of it will come to pass without rebuilding a strong, democratic, militant labor movement that can fight for the entire working class.

Conclusion: A Better Day

In early March 2019, Bernie Sanders kicked off his second campaign for the presidency in Brooklyn, New York, where he was born and raised. Snow blanketed the ground of Brooklyn College's East Quad. Thirteen thousand people braved the cold to hear Sanders speak about the tyranny of the rich and the need for a political revolution.

"I love the way Bernie talks about income inequality," said Phil Wynter, a forty-eight-year-old black man from Queens. "He directs the anger to who it's supposed to be directed to, which is the people with all the money and all the power."

"With Bernie, I understand why he aims his critique at the top," said Raul Hernandez, a twenty-nine-year-old from Elizabeth, New Jersey, whose family are immigrants from Colombia and Cuba. "Especially me being a minority in America, there are issues in our communities but they're issues that could be fixed with money. And we don't have a lot of it."

"Bernie tackles class head on and isn't afraid to bring it to the forefront," said Leen Dweik, a college student who lives in Manhattan and whose family comes from Palestine. "In most other candidates' cases it's a background issue at best. They're not willing to stand up and say that we have to address the issue of the 1 percent owning everything and controlling everybody else's lives."

The crowd was packed tight, shoulder to shoulder. Some people danced for warmth as music played over the loudspeakers, anxious for the main act to begin. But before Sanders spoke, others had their turn at the microphone. One of these speakers had been personally invited by Sanders on short notice.

"Good afternoon, brothers and sisters," he said. "My name is Scott Slawson. I'm the president of UE Local 506 of the United Electrical Radio Machine Workers of America. We represent seventeen hundred advanced manufacturing workers in the proud blue-collar town of Erie, Pennsylvania."

Slawson's union local was one of two on strike for a week against their new employers, the Wabtec Corporation, which had just taken over from General Electric. Workers were demanding a contract that would include decent compensation and labor practices—no rollbacks on the gains they'd made after eighty-two years of negotiating with GE.

"I want to say thank you to Senator Sanders for his unwavering support of our fight against Wabtec's attempts to destroy the living standards of Erie County, Pennsylvania," said Slawson. In February, Sanders had sent a letter to the CEO of Wabtec demanding that the company yield to workers' demands.

The crowd was getting riled up. Four hundred and thirty miles away, striking workers huddled around mobile phones, watching a livestream of the event from their picket lines.

Then something remarkable happened. "Today," said Slawson, "seventeen hundred families are standing on a picket line in freezing cold temperatures in Erie, Pennsylvania, saying 'We've had enough!'" And the crowd—people like Wynter, Hernandez, and Dweik, whose lives look in many respects very different from the striking Erie workers, but are in crucial ways the same—broke into a spontaneous chant. "Strike! Strike! Strike! Strike! Strike!"

This moment showed the transformative potential of Bernie Sanders's campaign. By directing popular anger toward the top and encouraging working people's resistance from below, Sanders's democratic socialist message can inspire people across lines of difference to unite in solidarity against their common enemy: the bosses who pay them too little, the landlords and insurance CEOs who charge them too much, and the politicians who stoke racism, xenophobia, and all kinds of bigotry while carrying water for the wealthiest members of our staggeringly unequal society at the expense of the working-class majority.

This transformative potential is the reason we have vigorously supported Bernie Sanders's campaigns for president. But we aren't naive. Electing a socialist, even to the highest office in the beating heart of global capitalism, won't solve the crises facing our nation and our world. We support Bernie Sanders not just because we agree with his redistributive policy proposals, but because we believe in the world-altering power of working people—power that Sanders himself has helped build through his campaign.

Socialists and everyone who wants equality and justice should pay close attention to what excites working people's passions, raises their class consciousness, and inspires them to dream of a better world—even if what we observe surprises us, like a socialist running for president on a class-struggle social democratic platform in the absence of an established socialist movement.

Whether Sanders wins or loses in 2020—and many people reading this book will know the answer already—the elected officials whose campaigns he inspired must carry the same kind of "not me, us" approach to their campaigns and, if they're victorious, to their office. More importantly, whatever happens with Sanders or those other politicians, the socialist movement is on stronger footing than it was before Sanders broke into the mainstream.

That said, there are no guarantees that socialism will remain a subject of curiosity or interest for the American working class, much less permeate the political culture. We may in fact have a very short window of opportunity to intervene and grow our movement. It's our responsibility, whatever happens in 2020, to take the baton from Sanders and run with it.

This book has been an attempt to inspire readers to take advantage of that opportunity as strategically as possible. One lesson we hope they will take away is the urgent necessity of a class-struggle approach to all our political action, both in the state and outside it. The purpose of socialist politics is to build working people's power. That has to include winning real material victories, but we can't celebrate those victories for long. As the history of social democracy reveals, resting on our laurels while capitalism persists is a recipe for the eventual erosion of our accomplishments.

Right now, we need to pick more of the kinds of fights we've chronicled in this book. We need more candidates running in class-struggle elections and pushing to decommodify basic goods in our lives like health care, higher education, and housing; more protests and strikes; more fights against the tiny minority in the capitalist class that has an active interest in squeezing as much out of everyone else as possible while destroying the planet we all live on, as well as an interest in stoking hatred and division throughout society.

And we need those candidates and those initiatives to all meet under one roof: a socialist organization. Not all of the people who join these fights will be socialists, but with a strong socialist organization, we'll be able to pull them together to build the kind of working-class strength that can transform the world.

We of this Age

We each have one life to live. We should spend it free and happy. To maintain a system that renders people miserable and unfree, for no other reason than the accrual of a huge amount of profits to a small number of people, is a crime.

We deserve education, for the knowledge produced cumulatively over centuries of human civilization belongs to all of humanity. We deserve health care, for social innovations in the treatment of ailments should not be withheld from the ailing in their time of need. We deserve high-quality, comfortable housing to live in, designed not to profit the few but to shelter the many. We deserve an end to racism, sexism, xenophobia, homophobia, and all other forms of oppression. We deserve pure air to breathe, clean water to drink, and the earth's miraculous bounty to appreciate and enjoy. We deserve bread, and roses too. We deserve art and beauty. We deserve free time. We deserve peace. We deserve to feel connected and valued. We deserve democracy, a true say in our own destiny.

We deserve the world. And we won't have it until capitalism ends.

It's daunting, this idea that socialists must keep struggling through conditions unforeseen, possibly for the rest of our lives. But from our perspective, as two people who are committed to the socialist movement, it's not a slog. In fact, that struggle is meaningful and nourishing. We have built some of the most beautiful friendships of our lives—including with each other—in the socialist movement. And in the pursuit of an elevated human condition alongside close friends and total strangers, we have discovered a feeling of connectedness to humanity that's nearly impossible to find elsewhere in our alienated society.

To be a socialist, engaged in this perpetual struggle, entails many frustrations and some personal sacrifice. But it is also enlivening, enriching, and inspiring. At times it can feel downright spiritual. In his speech delivered in Canton, Ohio, the one that landed him in jail, Debs captured this sentiment beautifully:

> I have regretted a thousand times that I can do so little for the movement that has done so much for me. The little that I am, the little that I am hoping to be, I owe to the Socialist movement. It has given me my ideas and ideals; my principles and convictions, and I would not exchange one of them for all of Rockefeller's bloodstained dollars.
>
> It has taught me how to serve—a lesson to me of priceless value. It has taught me the ecstasy in the handclasp of a comrade. It has enabled me to hold high communion with you, and made it possible for me to take my place side by side with you in the great struggle for the better

day; to multiply myself over and over again, to thrill with a fresh-born manhood; to feel life truly worthwhile; to open new avenues of vision; to spread out glorious vistas; to know that I am kin to all that throbs; to be class-conscious, and to realize that, regardless of nationality, race, creed, color or sex, every man, every woman who toils, who renders useful service, every member of the working class without an exception, is my comrade, my brother and sister—and that to serve them and their cause is the highest duty of my life.

Win or lose, what Bernie Sanders has accomplished in the last five years can't be overstated. He has invited hundreds of thousands, perhaps eventually millions of people to join in the fight for a humane and free world, and to come to know through their own actions the meaning of solidarity.

It's now the task of the reborn socialist movement to act boldly, intervene intelligently, and continue to invite people into that struggle, so that the potential of this moment isn't squandered.

It's our task to act with foresight and strategy, with passion and determination, to make the socialist movement popular and viable, and transform it into a credible threat to capitalism. It's our task to inspire the broad and diverse working class to dream of a different future, one where all people are truly created equal, where human life is valued above profit, where cooperation and compassion are the prevailing principles of social life, and where exploitation of person by person is a distant, shameful memory.

We've been handed this task at a time when the stakes are higher than ever, with a rising far right in the United States and globally, and climate change poised to wreak havoc across the planet. But we've also been handed this task in the midst of a once-in-a-lifetime opportunity. There has not been a better time to be a socialist in the United States in the last century. There hasn't been a more urgent time to join the socialist movement, either. So join us.

Acknowledgments

This book is the result of several years of intentional education, informal conversation, and real-time problem solving alongside comrades in the Democratic Socialists of America and at Jacobin. Thanks to everyone in DSA whom we've struggled alongside and learned from since 2016, in particular the members of DSA's Bread and Roses caucus.

Special thanks to everyone who read portions of the book and gave feedback: Eric Blanc, Neal Meyer, Lillian Osborne, Jeremy Gong, Robbie Nelson, Shawn Gude, Chris Maisano, Barry Eidlin, Aaron Taube, and Trish Kahle. Thanks too to Seth Ackerman for editing nearly all of our Jacobin pieces that we drew from for this book, and to Ella Mahony for being a close comrade.

Thanks to everyone at Verso, including Natascha Uhlmann, Mark Martin, and especially our editor, Ben Mabie, who was the first to hear and take our pitch for this book, gave wise editorial feedback that restructured it, and shepherded the entire project to the finish line.

We would be lost without the friendship and solidarity of so many other socialists, but we're particularly indebted to

Bhaskar Sunkara. Bhaskar built an institution, Jacobin, that first changed our politics, then changed our lives by taking a chance on both of us. We feel incredibly lucky to spend our days working for a project we believe in so deeply. Thanks as well to the rest of the Jacobin staff, whose politics we agree with and company we enjoy. And thank you to everyone who has fought like hell for Bernie Sanders.

Meagan would like to thank, above all, her number-one comrade, partner in all things, and favorite person, Hannah Klein. She also has eternal gratitude for those DSA comrades who have joined her at picket lines and weddings, on rainy canvasses and sunny vacations, through the highs of victory and lows of defeat. Special thanks to East Bay DSA's Jeremy Gong, Molly Armstrong, Johnny Pearson, Ari Marcantonio, Nick French, and Frances Reade, her compass in an ever-changing terrain. Finally, she would like to thank her family, and remember her grandmother Doris, who championed this book and passed away before she could read it.

Micah would like to thank Barry Eidlin for allowing us to incorporate part of their Labor Studies Journal article and for shaping the way Micah approaches the labor movement and social problems generally. Thank you to Chicago DSA for the comradeship and the Malort, and Shawn Gude and Anthony Quezada for being physically, emotionally, and politically close, and Miles Kampf-Lassin for being good. Thank you to Benjamin Balthaser, whose generous offer of his South Bend, Indiana apartment as a place to write this book was crucial. Thank you to Lillian Osborne, who put up with and supported him throughout the book-writing process. Thanks too to his brother Jacob, whose arguments ensure he never sinks too far into a leftist echo chamber, and his parents Bev and Bill, whose lifetime at home and in the church made him the person he is.

Bibliographic Essay

Rather than clutter the text with footnotes, we have written this bibliographic essay. Its purpose is to name the primary influences on each chapter and to suggest further reading. While we have made an attempt to acknowledge the sources of quotes and facts in the body of the text, this essay explores the broader ecosystem of books and articles that helped us develop the ideas in this book. We hope it will be useful for further socialist political education.

We wrote some of the articles we list here. We include them because they show how we have worked out the ideas in this book over the course of several years. We have noted the cases in which the text in this book has been adapted from our previously published articles.

Introduction

On the basics of class, capitalism, and socialism, our thinking has been greatly informed by the works of Erik Olin Wright, Ellen Meiksins Wood, Ralph Miliband, Vivek Chibber, and many more whose names will appear in the rest of this essay.

We're also indebted to the classic writings of Karl Marx, Friedrich Engels, Karl Kautsky, Vladimir Lenin, Leon Trotsky, and Rosa Luxemburg, and to interpretations of their life and works written by authors like David Harvey, Lars Lih, Tariq Ali, Irving Howe, and Isaac Deutscher.

If you're interested in further developing your own understanding of capitalism, we suggest starting with Vivek Chibber's *Jacobin* pamphlet series *The ABCs of Capitalism* and Ellen Meiksins Wood's *The Origins of Capitalism*. For clarifications on what exactly we mean by socialism, we recommend Michael Harrington's *Socialism* and *Socialism: Past and Future* and Bhaskar Sunkara's *The Socialist Manifesto: The Case for Radical Politics in an Age of Extreme Inequality*. Verso and *Jacobin* teamed up on *The ABCs of Socialism*, a collection of introductory essays by many of our favorite contemporary socialist writers.

We also recommend *How to Be an Anticapitalist in the Twenty-First Century*, by the late, great Marxist theorist of class, Erik Olin Wright. Wright's book serves as a powerful and lucid introductory critique of capitalism, as well as a helpful overview of dominant socialist strategies. For those particularly interested in how socialists can navigate, take, and wield state power, we recommend Ralph Miliband's *Marxism and Politics*.

For perspectives on the twentieth century, we recommend Mike Davis's *Prisoners of the American Dream* and David Harvey's *A Brief History of Neoliberalism*. The best argument against the pervasive misconception that the United States under capitalism is the land of opportunity is Barbara Ehrenreich's *Nickel and Dimed*.

Finally, you'll notice we cite *Jacobin* articles *a lot* in the rest of this essay. We are deeply indebted to *Jacobin*—it has been essential in shaping our politics and transforming us into the socialists we are today. In addition to helping produce the magazine, we religiously read it, and we hope you will, too.

1. The Man and the Movement

Many of the details of Bernie Sanders's political career come from his three books, *Outsider in the White House*, *Our Revolution*, and *Where We Go from Here: Two Years in the Resistance*. The *New York Times*'s primary writer assigned to Sanders, Sydney Ember, does not share our politics, but many of her pieces shed light on Sanders's life and career as well, including "Mayor and 'Foreign Minister': How Bernie Sanders Brought the Cold War to Burlington," "'I Did My Best to Stop American Foreign Policy': Bernie Sanders on the 1980s," and "Bernie Sanders Went to Canada, and a Dream of 'Medicare for All' Flourished."

 Other articles contributing to our understanding of Sanders's life include Michael Kruse's "Bernie Sanders Has a Secret" in *Politico*; Margaret Talbot's "Bernie Sanders, the Populist Prophet" in the *New Yorker*; Miles Kampf-Lassin's "What Chicago Taught Bernie" in *Jacobin*; Kevin J. Kelley's "Bernie's Bro: Working-Class Brooklyn Roots Shaped My Brother" in *Seven Days*; and Andrew Kaczynski and Nathan McDermott's "Bernie Sanders in the 1970s urged nationalization of most major industries" in CNN.

 Our perspective on the brutality of US intervention in Latin America in the twentieth century is informed by Stephen G. Rabe's *The Killing Zone: The United States Wages Cold War in Latin America* and Mark Danner's *The Massacre at El Mozote*. On the national movement against US intervention, see Hilary Goodfriend's "A Demand for Sanctuary" in *Jacobin*. On Sanders's activism against US intervention, see *Outsider in the White House* as well as Hilary Goodfriend's "Why Bernie Was Right to Oppose US Intervention in Central America" in *Jacobin*. On Sanders's foreign policy generally, see Daniel Bessner's "On Foreign Policy, Bernie Sanders Stands Alone" and Sarah Lazare's "Finding the Lesser Evil" in *Jacobin*.

The full text of Sanders's filibuster speech was published as a book called *The Speech: On Corporate Greed and the Decline of Our Middle Class.*

On the importance of political consistency over time, see Meagan Day and Micah Uetricht's "Riding the Fence on Medicare for All Isn't Smart Politics" in *Jacobin*. On Fox News accidentally and counterintuitively warming people up to socialism, see Meagan Day's "Fox News's Incredible 'Socialism' Self-Own" in *Jacobin*.

For an accessible and valuable early history of American socialism, read John Nichols's *The "S" Word: A Short History of an American Tradition . . . Socialism.* For more details on the American labor upsurges and socialist developments, see Jeremy Brecher's *Strike!*, Nelson Lichtenstein's *State of the Union,* and Paul Le Blanc's *A Short History of the U.S. Working Class.*

On Bernie Sanders and Eugene Debs, see Shawn Gude's "You Can Have Brandeis or You Can Have Debs" in *Jacobin*. For a general overview of Debs's life, see Ray Ginger's *The Bending Cross: A Biography of Eugene Victor Debs,* as well as Nick Salvatore's *Eugene Debs: Socialist and Citizen.* If you want a breezier Debs biography, read *Eugene V. Debs: A Graphic Biography* by Paul Buhle and Steve Max, illustrated by Noah Van Sciver.

On labor upsurges during the Great Depression, in addition to Brecher's *Strike!*, see Irving Bernstein, *The Turbulent Years:*

A History of the American Worker, 1933–1941; Frances Fox Piven and Richard Cloward's *Poor People's Movements: Why They Succeed, How They Fail*; and Mike Goldfield's "Worker Insurgency, Radical Organization, and New Deal Labor Legislation" in the *American Political Science Review*. For a gripping and politically astute account of the Minneapolis General Strike of 1934, read Ferrell Dobbs's *Teamster Rebellion*.

2. Class Struggle at the Ballot Box

On the uneven tilt of the playing field for leftists vying for power, see Ralph Miliband's *The State in Capitalist Society* and Vivek Chibber's *The ABCs of Capitalism*. On capital flight, see Kevin Young, Michael Schwartz, and Tarun Banerjee's "When Capitalists Go on Strike" in *Jacobin* and Charles Lindblom's "The Market As Prison," published in the *Journal of Politics*.

For a clear articulation of the concept of "class struggle elections," read the "Tasks for 2019" section on the website of the Bread and Roses caucus within DSA, of which we are members. For more on how the concept of class struggle elections relates to Bernie Sanders, see Meagan Day's "Bernie Sanders Wants You To Fight" and "What to Make of Warren's Policy Blitz" in *Jacobin*. On class struggle elections more broadly, read Megan Svoboda's "What Are Class Struggle Elections?" and Jack McShane's "Class-Struggle Politicians Are Organizers First, Legislators Second," both in the Bread and Roses caucus publication *The Call*.

For more on Rahm Emanuel, read Micah Uetricht's "Today and Forever, Rahm Emanuel is Garbage" in *Jacobin* and Rick Perlstein's "The Sudden But Well-Deserved Fall of Rahm Emanuel" in the *New Yorker*.

On Sanders's strategic antagonism of billionaires, see "CEOs vs. Workers" and "Bernie Sanders: The Boss's Worst Nightmare," both by Meagan Day, and Micah Uetricht's "Pointing the Finger at Jeff Bezos Worked," all published in *Jacobin*.

For more on Sanders's use of his campaign infrastructure to support strikes and protests, see Dave Jamieson's "Bernie Sanders Used His Campaign Data To Drive Turnout On Strike Picket Lines" in the *Huffington Post*; Jeff Schuhrke's "Did You Get a Text Inviting You to a Picket Line? It Might Be from Bernie Sanders" in *In These Times*; and Holly Otterbein's "What Sanders' political revolution looks like in real life" in *Politico*.

The piece positing that Alexandria Ocasio-Cortez had begun to play nice with the Democrats is Catie Edmondson's "How Alexandria Ocasio-Cortez Learned to Play by Washington's Rules" in the *New York Times*. On the importance of Ocasio-Cortez's endorsement of Sanders, see Meagan Day and Nick French's "AOC's Endorsement of Bernie Makes Perfect Sense" in *Jacobin*. The dramatic inside story of the endorsement is from Alex Thompson and Holly Otterbein's "How Bernie won a prized endorsement from his hospital bed" in *Politico*.

For more on DSA's past and present, see Jeff Stein's "9 questions about the Democratic Socialists of America you were too embarrassed to ask" in *Vox*; Maurice Isserman's biography of DSA's founder, *The Other American: The Life of Michael Harrington*; and Meagan Day's "Tribunes for Socialism: Reflections on DSA and Electoral Politics" in Verso's edited collection *Socialist Strategy and Electoral Politics*.

Interviews with DSA members Nick Conder, Kristen Schall, Tim Higginbotham, Bryan LaVergne, Madeline Detelich, and Oren Schweitzer were conducted by Meagan. The interview with Aaron Taube was conducted by Micah.

3. Socialists in Action

Both of us have learned a great deal about the socialist electoral movement by interviewing candidates and socialist elected officials for *Jacobin*. Meagan has interviewed Kshama Sawant, Jovanka Beckles, Julia Salazar, Jumaane Williams, Dean Preston, Franklin Bynum, Lee Carter, Candi CdeBaca, Lililiana Rivera Baiman, Paige Kreisman, Chesa Boudin, Tom Gallagher, and others. Micah has interviewed Julia Salazar, Carlos Rosa, Rossana Rodriguez, Jeanette Taylor, Ugo Okere, Heidi Sloan, Anthony Clark, and Cathy Kunkel.

The most important source of insight into Chicago's elections was Micah's own participation in them, especially in the Rossana Rodriguez-Sanchez and Carlos Rosa campaigns, and conversations with participants in the elections. Thanks especially to Alex Han, Lillian Osborne, and all the DSA activists who worked on these campaigns. Parts of the Chicago section first appeared as "Today, Chicago. Tomorrow, Your City," in the summer 2019 issue of DSA's magazine *Democratic Left*. For more on the socialist victories in Chicago, read Micah Uetricht's "America's socialist surge is going strong in Chicago" in the *Guardian* and "A Good Night for Chicago Socialists" in *Jacobin*. See also Will Bloom's "A Socialist Wave in Chicago" in Jacobin, Lucie Macias and Leonard Pierce's "Democratic socialists: No more business as usual in Chicago" in the *Chicago Tribune*, and Steve Weishampel's "Electoral Victories in Chicago: How the Socialist Caucus Was Built" in *Midwest Socialist*. Marianela D'Aprile's interview of Lillian Osborne in *Socialist Forum*, "Chicago's Red Wave," is also useful.

On the historical background of the Chicago socialist electoral upsurge, see Micah Uetricht's *Strike for America: Chicago*

Teachers Against Austerity, and Miles Kampf-Lassin's "Chicago's Political Revolution" in *In These Times*. The op-ed authored by all six Chicago socialist aldermen and published in the *Chicago Sun-Times* is titled "If we care enough about Chicago's children, the money is there for the schools they deserve."

Like Micah, Meagan's primary source for the section on socialist politics in the East Bay is her personal participation as a member of East Bay DSA. Meagan wrote an early version of her observations in the essay "Tribunes for Socialism: Reflections on DSA and Electoral Politics" in Verso's edited collection *Socialist Strategy and Electoral Politics*. For more on Jovanka Beckles, see her 2018 campaign website, which at the time of this book's publication is still live at jovanka.org. Pay special attention to her platform, the most radical in California in 2018.

A history of Beckles and the Richmond Progressive Alliance's heroic fight against Chevron can be read in Steve Early's book *Refinery Town: Big Oil, Big Money, and the Remaking of an American City*. For more on Beckles, see the interview Meagan conducted with her for *Jacobin* titled "We Need a New Economy That Works for the Many," and an op-ed that Beckles herself wrote for *Jacobin* titled "Solving California's Housing Crisis." Don't forget to visit East Bay DSA's Buffy Wicks website, buffywicks.money.

East Bay Majority, the official publication of East Bay DSA, is a good source for information on the Oakland teachers' strike, and is itself a part of the story told in this chapter. See, for example, Nick French's *Majority* article "The Oakland school crisis and the billionaires who caused it," Joel Jordan's "From the Bay to LA, teachers and families are fighting the same enemies," and Katie Ferrari's multi-part series "Everything you need to know about the proposed Oakland school closures."

For more on the Oakland teachers' strike, read Eric Blanc's "Oakland Teachers Are Striking Against Billionaire Privatizers" and "Why Oakland's Striking Teachers Won," both in *Jacobin*. Also read Meagan Day's interview with teacher Tim Marshall for *Jacobin*, "'We're Fighting a Mean-Spirited and Anti-democratic Attack on Public Education.'"

The details of New York's electoral victories, battle with Amazon, and affordable housing victories came from Nicky Woolf's "'The Hunger Games for cities' – inside the Amazon HQ2 bid process" in the *New Statesman*; Michael Greenberg's "A Historic Win for New York Tenants" in the *New York Review of Books*; Vivian Wang's "Democratic Insurgents Topple 6 New York Senate Incumbents" in the *New York Times*; Samuel Stein's "Tenants Won This Round" in *Jacobin*; an interview with Susan Kang conducted by Ella Mahony for *Jacobin* titled "How New York Politics Has Changed"; and Liza Featherstone's "How the NYC Left Took on Amazon and Won" in *Jacobin*. We are also indebted to Cea Weaver and Aaron Taube for their invaluable interviews with Micah.

4. The Dirty Break

Our ideas about what the path to socialism looks like specifically in the United States have been shaped by Vivek Chibber's "Our Road to Power" in *Jacobin*, Chris Maisano's "Which Way to Socialism?" in *The Call*, and Eric Blanc's "Why Kautsky Was Right (and Why You Should Care)" in *Jacobin*. Though it isn't specifically about the United States, the final chapter of Ralph Miliband's *Marxism and Politics* is useful, too.

The phrase "the dirty break" was coined by Eric Blanc in his *Jacobin* essay "The Ballot and the Break." Since then he has written and debated extensively on this topic, and his contributions have informed our thinking. See his essays "Socialists, Democrats, and the Dirty Break" and "On History and the Dirty Break" in *Socialist Worker*. For more on democratic reforms and class struggle, read Chris Maisano's "Bernie's Political Revolution Requires Radical Democratic Reform" and Adaner Usmani's "To Save Democracy, We Need Class Struggle."

On details about the promise and failures of numerous socialist governments around the world, Bhaskar Sunkara's *The Socialist Manifesto* is excellent. On France and the Mitterrand government, see Jonah Birch's "The Many Lives of Francois Mitterrand" in *Jacobin*. On Chile, see Ralph Miliband's indispensable essay "The Coup in Chile."

The title of the "phantom limb" section of this chapter is taken from Barry Eidlin's *Jacobin* essay of the same name. Many of the arguments in this section come from Eidlin, too—especially the United States and Canada comparisons, which Eidlin makes in his book *Labor and the Class Idea in the United States and Canada*. Also invaluable is his *Jacobin* essay "From Class to Special Interest."

All of the information in this chapter about campaign and election financing comes from Open Secrets, which is a site we recommend exploring if you want to grasp the extent of capitalists' influence over US politics.

Seth Ackerman's *Jacobin* essay "A Blueprint for a New Party" has been very influential to us and others in DSA in describing both what's wrong with the Democratic Party and why we can't just start a new party and do away with them. Several of the examples cited in this section, including the anecdote about the Arizona Libertarians and the Theodore Lowi quote, come from this essay.

On the history of the Labor Party, see Derek Seidman's interview with Mark Dudzic in *Jacobin*, "What Happened to the Labor Party?" as well as Les Leopold's biography of Tony Mazzocchi, *The Man Who Hated Work and Loved Labor.*

The section on realignment was strongly influenced by Paul Heideman's *Jacobin* essay "It's Their Party," and several quotes in this section, such as the one from Cleveland Sellers, come from that essay. The anecdotes about Bill Clinton at Stone Mountain and the "superpredators" comment come from Nathan Robinson, *Superpredator: Bill Clinton's Use and Abuse of Black America.* On the need for an electoral vehicle beyond Our Revolution, see Micah Uetricht's "The World Turned Upside Down: 'Our Revolution,' Trump Triumphant, and the Remaking of the Democratic Party" in *New Labor Forum.*

On the practice of internal democracy, see Mike Parker and Martha Gruelle, *Democracy Is Power.* We are particularly indebted to Parker for his insights on this issue over the years within DSA.

5. *Engines of Solidarity*

For an introduction to Sweden's social democracy and the country's history of class struggle and socialist politics, we recommend the chapter on Sweden in Bhaskar Sunkara's *The Socialist Manifesto: The Case for Radical Politics in an Era of Extreme Inequality.* For a more in-depth perspective, see Carly Elizabeth Schall's *The Rise and Fall of the Miraculous Welfare Machine.*

If you just can't get enough about the history of Swedish social democracy, hoo boy—*Jacobin* is the magazine for you. See Kjell Östberg's "Was Sweden Headed Toward Socialism in the 1970s?", Peter Gowan and Mio Tastas Viktorsson's "Revisiting the Meidner Plan," Peter Gowan's "The Radical Reformist," and an interview with Erik Bengtsson titled "Before Sweden Was Social-Democratic."

On the limits of social democracy, start with Marcel Liebman and Ralph Miliband's classic essay "Beyond Social Democracy," which has been reprinted in *Jacobin*, Robert Brenner's "The Problem of Reformism" in *Against the Current*, and Leo Panitch's "The Impasse of Social Democratic Politics." We also recommend Peter Frase's "Social Democracy's Breaking Point," Michael McCarthy's "Democratic Socialism Isn't Social Democracy," Chris Maisano's "Social Democracy's Incomplete Legacy," and Joe Schwartz and Bhaskar Sunkara's "Social Democracy Is Good. But Not Good Enough," all in *Jacobin*.

On the commitment to democracy at the heart of the socialist project, we recommend Shawn Gude's "Democratic Socialism Is About Democracy," Barry Eidlin's "Why I'm A Socialist," both in *Jacobin*. Chris Maisano's writings on the question of democracy are invaluable, including his *Jacobin* essays "Is Democracy Doomed?" and "Bernie's Political Revolution Requires Radical Democratic Reform," and his *Catalyst* essay "Democracy's Morbid Symptoms."

On capitalism's body count, read Mike Davis's book *Late Victorian Holocausts: El Niño Famines and the Making of the Third World*. See also Meagan Day's interview with Mike Davis in *Jacobin*, "Mike Davis on the Crimes of Socialism and Capitalism."

For a view of what socialism can look like, read Sam Gindin's essay "Socialism for Realists" in *Catalyst*. For more on the relationship between planning and markets under socialism, see Seth Ackerman's "The Red and the Black" in *Jacobin*.

We think it's imperative that socialists who want to continue their political education read Rosa Luxemburg's "Reform or Revolution." We also recommend André Gorz's "Reform and Revolution." There's never any harm in reading Vladimir Lenin's "'Left-Wing' Communism: An Infantile Disorder," either.

For more on Bernie Sanders, Franklin Delano Roosevelt, and the legacy of the New Deal, we recommend Seth Ackerman's "Why Bernie Talks About the New Deal," and an interview by Micah with Ackerman titled "What Bernie Sees in the New Deal," both in *Jacobin*.

The term "engines of solidarity" was coined by Robbie Nelson in his *Jacobin* article of the same name. Meagan Day has also written extensively in *Jacobin* about means testing and universality, including "Targeted Social Programs Make Easy Targets," "Why We Need Free College for Everyone— Even Rich People," "The US Could Have A Welfare State—But We Don't," "Elizabeth Warren and Taxes: This Shouldn't Be So Hard," "The Bureaucratic Nightmare of Incrementalism," and "Austerity By Paperwork."

On the Green New Deal, begin with *A Planet to Win: Why We Need a Green New Deal* by Kate Aronoff, Alyssa Battistoni, Daniel Aldana Cohen, and Thea Riofrancos. See also Matt Huber's essay in *Catalyst*, "Ecological Politics for the Working Class," and the *Socialist Forum* essay "A Class Struggle Strategy for a Green New Deal." written by Keith Brower-Brown, Jeremy Gong, Matt Huber, and Jamie Munro. *Jacobin*'s Green New Deal series has been invaluable in shaping our thinking on the topic.

One of the best arguments in favor of socialism in general and full employment in particular is, surprisingly, written by Albert Einstein. It's called "Why Socialism?" and was published in the *Monthly Review* in 1959.

6. *Rank-and-File Revolution*

A significant portion of this chapter was adapted from Micah
Uetricht and Barry Eidlin's "US Union Revitalization and the
Missing 'Militant Minority,'" published in *Labor Studies
Journal*. That article was the product of a year's worth of
graduate study with Eidlin, whose ideas about labor and social
movements and approach to analyzing social problems generally have been incredibly influential to Micah. Special thanks
to Barry for allowing the adaptation of the article here.

The single thinker who has shaped our ideas about the
labor movement more than anyone else is Kim Moody.
Particularly recommended are *An Injury to All: The Decline
of American Unionism* for an overview of the history of the
US labor movement; *On New Terrain: How Capital Is
Shaping the Battleground of Class War* for a strategic analysis
of the American economy and opportunities for organizing;
and "The Rank and File Strategy" for an explanation of the
why and how of said strategy. The quote at the end of this
chapter about socialist humility comes from his essay collection *In Solidarity: Essays on Working-Class Organization in the
United States*.

On the question of why workers are key for socialists, Vivek
Chibber has written many articles for *Jacobin*: "Why We Still
Talk about the Working Class"; "Workers Hold the Keys" (an
interview with Jason Farbman); and "Why the Working Class?"

For a fun read of nearly all the times American workers
have walked off the job en masse over the past century and
a half, see Jeremy Brecher's *Strike!* For the best contemporary
overview of today's labor movement, see Jane McAlevey's *No
Shortcuts: Organizing for Power in the New Gilded Age*. On
the teachers strike wave, see Eric Blanc's dozens of articles

for *Jacobin* and his book *Red State Revolt: The Teachers' Strike Wave and Working-Class Politics* and Micah Uetricht's *Strike for America: Chicago Teachers against Austerity*. Blanc's book and articles are also important in discussing the extent to which the Sanders campaign helped touch off the teachers' strikes.

On the history of Communists and other radicals in the American labor movement, there is a long bibliography in "US Union Revitalization and the Missing 'Militant Minority'" by Uetricht and Eidlin. But some key readings on this topic include Judith Stepan-Norris and Maurice Zeitlin's *Left Out: Reds and America's Industrial Unions*; Michael Kimeldorf's *Reds or Rackets?: The Making of Radical and Conservative Unions on the Waterfront*; Roger Horowitz's *"Negro and White, Unite and Fight!": A Social History of Industrial Unionism in Meatpacking, 1930–90*; *Labor and Communism*, by Bert Cochran; Roger Keeran's *The Communist Party and the Auto Workers' Unions*; Michael Goldfield's "Worker Insurgency, Radical Organization, and New Deal Labor Legislation" in *The American Political Science Review*; and Mike Davis's *Prisoners of the American Dream: Politics and Economy in the History of the US Working Class*.

The organization that is dedicated to rebuilding the "militant minority" in the United States is Labor Notes—not only through their eponymous magazine, but also through their biennial conference, regional trainings, and by generally serving as a resource to connect militant rank and filers around the country and the world. You should check them out at labornotes.org, attend their national conferences in Chicago, and support them.

On the question of unions and bureaucracy, see Robert Brenner's "The Paradox of Social Democracy," available at versobooks.com. Some of these paradoxes played out during the 2016 election as revealed by WikiLeaks, which *Buzzfeed*'s Cora Lewis was the first to report on in "The Clinton Campaign's Labor Hierarchy, from Walmart Workers to Union Chiefs." Branko Marcetic dug up further dirt in "Leaks Show Machinists' Union President Secretly Moved Up Endorsement Vote to Help Clinton" in *In These Times*.

On the history of Teamsters for a Democratic Union, see Dan La Botz's chapter "The Tumultuous Teamsters in the 1970s" in *Rebel Rank and File* (edited by Aaron Brenner, Rob Brenner, and Cal Winslow) and Joe Allen's many articles on the history of TDU and on Ron Carey in *Jacobin*.

Meagan Day has interviewed many rank-and-file organizers for *Jacobin,* ranging from San Francisco brewers ("'There Wouldn't Be Craft Beer If It Weren't for Us'") to Indianapolis janitors ("'They Don't Understand the Value of Life'") to New York City tech and art world workers ("A Union Is an Equalization of Power"; "Fight at the Museum"). These conversations have heavily influenced her perspective.

On dirty industries and the Green New Deal, historian Trish Kahle's work has been critical. She has written about this at length for *Jacobin*, in articles such as "Rank and File Environmentalism" and "Taking On the Fossil Fuel Bosses," as well as in her dissertation "The Graveyard Shift: Mining Democracy in an Age of Energy Crisis, 1963–1981." On a class-struggle strategy to win a Green New Deal, see Matt Huber's "Ecological Politics for the Working Class" in *Catalyst* and "A Real Green New Deal Means Class Struggle" by Matt Huber, Jeremy Gong, Keith Brower Brown, and Jamie Munro in *Socialist Forum*. Details on the Northern Ireland shipyard workers who occupied their factory come from Lauren Gurley in *Vice*.

Conclusion

All of the interviews with Bernie supporters at his rally in Brooklyn were conducted by Meagan and first published in the article "Among the Brooklyn Bernie Bros" in *Jacobin*.

Eugene Debs's Canton Speech is the best socialist speech ever delivered on US soil. Every American socialist should read it in full at least once, and ideally revisit it often. If you're looking for an audio dramatization of the Canton Speech, you're in luck: Bernie Sanders can be heard reciting excerpts from it in his 1979 documentary about Debs. *Jacobin* published the full documentary on YouTube under the title "Bernie Sanders—Eugene Debs Documentary—1979." The segment where Sanders reads from the Canton Speech also appears in a moving video created by Luke Thibault titled "Bernie Sanders and Eugene Debs," published to social media in the heat of Bernie's 2020 presidential campaign by the Democratic Socialists of America.